Smart WORKSHOP *solutions*

Building Workstations, Jigs, and Accessories
to Improve Your Shop

PAUL ANTHONY

The Taunton Press

The Taunton Press
Inspiration for hands-on living®

The Taunton Press, Inc., 63 South Main Street, PO Box 5506, Newtown, CT 06470-5506
e-mail: tp@taunton.com

Distributed by Publishers Group West

EDITOR: Stefanie Ramp
COVER DESIGN: Howard Grossman
INTERIOR DESIGN: Lori Wendin
LAYOUT: Marta Strait
ILLUSTRATOR: Melanie Powell
PHOTOGRAPHER: Paul Anthony

Library of Congress Cataloging-in-Publication Data

Anthony, Paul, 1954-
    Smart workshop solutions : building workstations, jigs, and
accessories to improve your shop / Paul Anthony.
        p. cm.
    ISBN 1-56158-578-5
    1. Workshops--Equipment and supplies--Design and construction. I.
Title.
    TT153.A58 2003
    684'.08--dc21

                                                    2003007857

Printed in the United States of America
10 9 8 7 6 5 4 3 2

The following manufacturers/names appearing in *Smart Workshop Solutions* are trademarks: Accuride®, Adjust-A-Bench, Delta®, Fast Trak, Makita®, Masonite®, Melamine®, Porter Cable®, Rockler®, and Woodcraft®.

WORKING WITH WOOD IS INHERENTLY DANGEROUS. Using hand or power tools improperly or ignoring safety practices can lead to permanent injury or even death. Don't try to perform operations you learn about here (or elsewhere) unless you're certain they are safe for you. If something about an operation doesn't feel right, don't do it. Look for another way. We want you to enjoy the craft, so please keep safety foremost in your mind whenever you're in the shop.

To Mom and Dad, for all your love and support throughout the years

ACKNOWLEDGMENTS

THANKS TO THE STAFF AT THE TAUNTON PRESS for their good work throughout the creation of this book. I don't know how she does it, but Executive Editor Helen Albert always manages to work through difficulties with creativity and grace. Her editorial assistant, Jenny Peters, is as reliable as they come, and Managing Editor Carolyn Mandarano is always a pleasure to deal with. A special debt of gratitude goes to my editor, Stefanie Ramp, for her patience and meticulous work, as well as her humor and determination during the incessant eleventh-hour computer glitches and crashes.

This book would not be a reality without the help of all of the woodworkers who contributed their time and designs to it. It was a blast to visit the shops and homes of such a good-hearted, gracious bunch of folks. Thanks to Ken Burton, Craig Bentzley, Brian Boggs, Mike Callihan, Bill Hylton, Fred Matlack, Tony O'Malley, Andy Rae, Larry Seachrist, Walt Segl, Don Weber, and Bob Whitley. Special thanks to Ric Hanisch, Andy, and Fred for behind-the-scenes consultation and to Craig for going the extra mile when help was needed.

Last, but certainly not least, I couldn't have done this without the help and encouragement of my lovely wife, Jeanie.

CONTENTS

INTRODUCTION

TIME SPENT in the workshop is the most enjoyable part of the day for many woodworkers, whether amateur or professional. In fact, many of us have a sort of ongoing love affair with the shop because it's our place of creativity and refuge. It's where we make these beautiful, useful things that last for generations and where we go to recharge ourselves, surrounded by wood, projects, and tools.

If you're a woodworker, it's a good bet you love tools. That's a good reason to have your shop in shape, as it's the biggest tool you have. It pays to keep it fine-tuned and operating as efficiently as your saws and planes. An unruly shop can cause you grief as you hunt for that bit for the third time or screw up a cut because your quick-'n'-easy outfeed support fell over again. A well-tuned shop allows you to glide from one process to another, getting much more done and enjoying it more.

Chances are that no matter how well your shop is organized, you've got improvements floating around in your head as you work. Maybe the thought of a new lumber rack sprung to mind when you tripped over that pile of boards last week. Perhaps that recent back twinge from hoisting your "portable" planer is triggering the "tool-stand design" cortex of your woodworker brain. Or maybe you're just finally reaching the sad conclusion that you're no longer the young acrobat capable of traversing your overstuffed shop with only minor injuries.

Whatever the case, there is no shortage of good shop-improvement projects to minimize your wrestling bouts with tools and stock. To that end, this book offers designs for shop accessories such as lumber racks, clamp racks, outfeed and assembly tables, and tool-storage solutions. What's more, you'll find designs for various shop workstations dedicated to particular woodworking processes. Workstations are not only the best approach to efficient production, but they also make woodworking more enjoyable and safe.

Whether a workstation is dedicated to sharpening, drilling, sawing, assembling, or sanding, it includes all of the tools, supplies, and space you'll need to perform a particular process. For example, a sharpening station usually includes a grinder and honing stones placed at the appropriate working height, with a wheel dresser, water for cooling, and any grinding and honing jigs nearby. No matter how it is configured, a workstation that provides a ready-to-go work platform with all of the necessary tools and supplies close at hand will pay off big dividends in efficiency and quality of work.

So have at it. I think you'll find that the projects in this book will make your time in the shop more productive and enjoyable. Just don't forget to step outside for some sunshine once in a while.

Craig Bentzley's shop is a model of compact efficiency. Thoughtfully designed storage and carefully positioned machines create an environment for smooth production of woodworking projects.

SMART WORKSHOP SOLUTIONS

WHETHER YOUR WORKSHOP is in a garage, a basement, or a warehouse, organization and efficiency matter. And they matter to both professionals and recreational woodworkers alike, because a well-organized, properly outfitted shop pays off big dividends in terms of both productivity and enjoyment.

The whole idea of organization and efficiency is to make life in the shop easier and more fun. Woodworking is challenging enough without building difficulties into the process by poorly arranging tools and using shoddy shop fixtures and accessories. It's funny—I've spoken to hobbyist woodworkers who seem to think that efficiency only matters to professionals who are trying to crank work out the door. But efficiency matters to everyone. Woodworking tends to be labor intensive, and if you're going to get projects done, you can't waste a lot of time diddling with your machines and searching fruitlessly for misplaced tools and supplies. After all, if you're going to get points for that "honey-do" cabinet for the spouse, you have to actually hand over the goods sometime.

There are a number of approaches to increasing efficiency in the shop, but the most important involves thoughtful shop layout and appropriate fixtures and workstations. The way your machines and other tools are placed in relation to each other can save a lot of wasted steps and aggravation throughout the workday. Well-designed fixtures such as wood racks and clamp racks can ease access to materials and tools, saving you a lot of time during project layout and assembly. Carefully conceived workstations condense into one area almost everything you need for a process, maximizing your time and energy.

Small shops benefit especially from organization because space is at such a premium. When every tool has its place, work goes more smoothly. Keep in mind that an organized shop doesn't have to be uncomfortably neat. I've visited countless shops over the years, and every one has a style of its own. Clearly, a shop doesn't have to be pretty to produce beautiful work. I've seen plenty of amazing work emerge from some crude-looking shops, but the more productive of those shops were organized in their own way and carefully tailored to the nature of the work produced there.

Tool Arrangement and Work Flow

To streamline your work, begin by taking a close look at your work processes. Work flow usually begins with board layout near the wood storage area, which is best located near the shop's loading entrance. After boards are laid out for initial rough cutting, they are generally crosscut on a nearby radial-arm saw or sliding crosscut miter (SCM) saw. After that, the pieces usually move to the jointer for face jointing and then to the planer for thicknessing. Next, the work may be routed back to the jointer for edge jointing and then to the table saw for ripping to final width. The final cuts involve crosscutting to length at the table saw, radial-arm saw, or SCM saw.

Because these milling processes are so closely related, it's important to locate the crosscut saw, jointer, planer, and table saw in close proximity to one another. When arranging or rearranging a shop to maximize work flow, it's helpful to make a scaled drawing of the floor plan, using cutouts of your tools to play with different scenarios (see photo A). A tight shop space can call for creative tool placement. Sometimes smaller machines can be mounted directly to the wall—perhaps above another machine (see photos B and C).

When working on a project, you also need staging, which simply means a place to stack the pieces in process. There are several approaches to this, including installing a bench near a tool, using sawhorses, or employing a portable cart (see photo D). If your space is tight, it makes sense to demand double duty from the surfaces you have. For example, my jointer sits to the right of my table saw, and I use the table-saw extension tables as a staging area for holding the stock being jointed (see photo E on p. 8).

To develop the best work flow for your particular shop, pay close attention to areas where snags exist. Perhaps simply adding a strategically placed benchtop or other form of staging will expedite matters. But some-

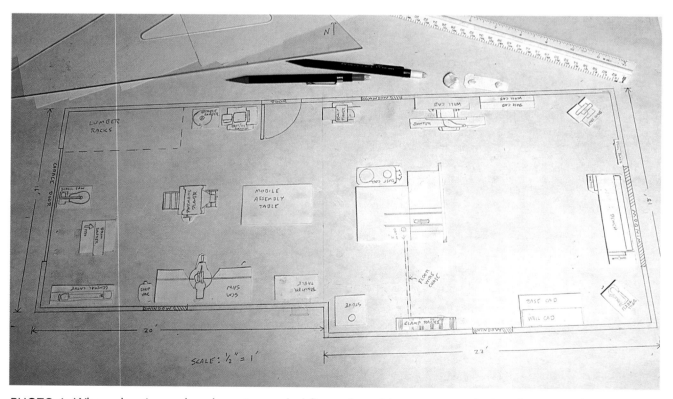

PHOTO A: When planning a shop layout, a scaled floor plan with separate scaled tool cutouts allow playing with machine and shop-cabinet placement to create an efficient work flow throughout the shop.

PHOTOS B AND C:
Space is at a pre-
mium in Fred
Matlack's tiny shop,
so he mounted his
portable planer on a
platform fixed to the
wall above his table
saw's side extension
table (far left photo).
His benchtop belt
sander rests on sup-
ports screwed to
wall studs behind
his jointer (near left
photo).

times the best solution is to temporarily
move a machine to an existing staging area,
rather than the other way around. Many
kinds of commercial mobile bases are available these days (see photo F on p. 8), or you
can simply add casters to a shopmade base.
Making machines mobile is one of the best
ways to build flexibility into any shop, large
or small. Speaking of mobility, don't forget
that you'll need a way to move large projects
in process around the shop. The simple solution for that is to employ shopmade dollies
with casters (see photo G on p. 8).

Fixtures and Workstations

Some of the best improvements you can
make to a shop involve creating appropriate
fixtures and workstations. This is the fun stuff
that can help you glide through your workday. Fixtures include things like clamp racks,
wood racks, tool cabinets, and auxiliary
machine tables. Workstations are personal
configurations that often consist of custom-
made cabinets, stands, and auxiliary tables

PHOTO D: Ken Burton's mobile parts cart is outfitted with
removable outriggers for performing double duty as an
auxiliary support when feeding sheets of plywood onto the
table saw.

PHOTO E: Locating a jointer near a table saw makes for efficient milling and allows use of the table-saw wing as staging for workpieces being jointed.

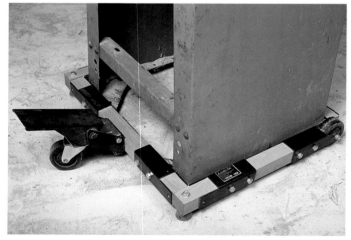

PHOTO F: A wide variety of mobile bases are available for woodworking machines. Delta® makes a kit that consists of corner brackets and a lift wheel to which you add suitable shopmade rails.

PHOTO G: Bob Whitley keeps a shelf full of dollies on hand for moving large workpieces in process around the shop.

suited to a particular tool or process. A well-designed workstation will keep all necessary tools and accessories close at hand and will include features like built-in adjustable stops for quick, accurate setups of cuts.

A workstation isn't necessarily a separate, discrete project unto itself; it often comprises a number of components placed in proper relation to a particular piece of equipment. A table-saw station, for instance, might include extension tables with a cabinet underneath for storing blades, wrenches, push sticks, and table-saw jigs. In addition, several types of auxiliary rip fences and a crosscut sled might be part of the package. A drilling station, configured around a drill press, might feature a custom drill-press table, as well as a cabinet for bits, countersinks, and boring vises. A sharpening station will include a grinder and a water tray for honing stones, as well as a strong inspection light (see photo H).

A workstation doesn't have to be fancy. It may be as simple as a base cabinet built

PHOTO H: A workstation should include everything needed for a particular process. Andy Rae's sharpening station consists of a grinder, a stone pond, and a cabinet to house various sharpening jigs. Note that the grinder is placed at a comfortable height and is shrouded to prevent it from scattering metal particles.

PHOTO I: Workstations don't have to be fancy, just functional. This disk-sander cabinet with its upper shelf does triple duty as a tool stand, a storage cabinet, and a small staging platform.

TIP

It's often wise to buy
an extra wrench,
screwdriver, or
square for use at a
specific station,
rather than crossing
the shop to dig
through your toolbox
for it. A couple of
bucks spent here can
save you a lot
of steps over the
years. For example,
an extra 4-in. machin-
ist's square lives by
my jointer for regular
fine-tuning of the
fence. At my band-
saw, I keep a dedicat-
ed Allen wrench for
resetting the guide
blocks after a blade
change.

specifically to accommodate a particular tool
(see photo I on p. 9). Some tools, such as the
bandsaw, don't need a lot of storage for
accessories. Instead, you can use magnets to
keep the necessary blade-changing tools close
at hand (see photo J).

You'll find some great workstation projects in these pages, but you may well want to
modify a design to suit your particular needs
or machine. Just remember when designing
storage for a workstation that it's best to first
gather all of the intended contents and make
sure there's a place for everything. Then
incorporate space for any future acquisitions.

Materials

All of the projects in this book are made
from solid wood, hardwood plywood,
and/or medium-density fiberboard (MDF)
(see photo K on facing page). Most of the
projects incorporate some hardware, ranging
from screws and hinges to drawer slides and
casters. None of the stuff is hard to find. In
fact, many projects in this book were made
from whatever materials were on hand.

In most cases, common domestic species
of wood were used for these projects. These
are shop projects, after all, and don't need to
be very fancy. However, you may want to use
pretty woods for the occasional project to
showcase your woodworking skills for clients
and friends. Like craftsmen of old who often
represented their skills in their toolboxes,
your shop fixtures and furniture say a lot
about your work. As Craig Bentzley points
out, clients who visit his shop when he's
between commissions can see a reflection of
his skills in his shop itself, even if there is no
project in process at the time.

Solid wood is available from lumber suppliers, mills, and home-supply centers.
Hardwood plywood can be purchased at
some home-supply centers and wood dealers. You may also be able to buy it from a
friendly commercial cabinet shop. All of the
hardware is either available at your local
hardware store or home-supply center or
through the mail-order suppliers listed in
Sources on p. 172.

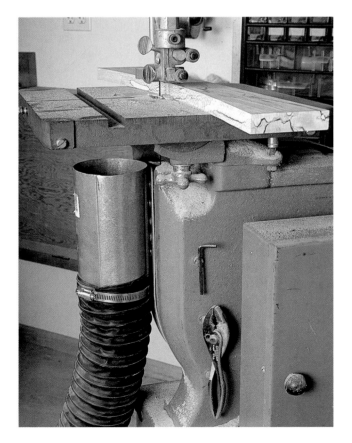

PHOTO J: Magnets make
great holders for companion
tools at machines. The Allen
wrench and pliers on this
bandsaw are used whenever
a blade is changed. Notice
that magnets also provide a
way to attach a section of
metal dust-collection pipe
so that it can be quickly
disconnected.

Solid wood

Solid wood is used in many of these projects for face frames, rails, legs, and other parts. Although these are shop projects—not furniture for the home—it's still important to use well-seasoned lumber that is sound and free of cracks and checks. That said, you don't need the same sort of premium lumber that you would use for furniture, and it's not as critical that the wood color and grain patterns be as consistent. These projects can present a good opportunity to use up leftover wood from previous furniture projects.

Hardwood plywood

Plywood has certain advantages over solid wood, the primary one being that it is stable, so you don't have to worry about accommodating wood movement. You can fit plywood panels snugly into frames or drawer-side grooves without worry of them expanding and blowing joints apart.

Hardwood plywood isn't cheap but, on a square-foot basis, it's typically less expensive than solid wood. Stay away from construction-grade plywood, as it is often full of voids and prone to warping and delamination. Some plywood dealers offer "shop-grade" hardwood plywood, which is less expensive because of its minor defects. It's the perfect economy material for many shop projects.

MDF

MDF is a high-grade form of particleboard. Unlike typical particleboard, MDF is dense, flat, smooth, and stable. It can be used in many cases as an inexpensive alternative to hardwood plywood. In fact, MDF is sometimes used as a substrate for high-grade veneer panels, such as those used in the tool cabinet in chapter 9. MDF is preferable to plywood for applications that require extreme flatness, such as router tabletops and jig parts.

Like any material, MDF does have its disadvantages. First off, it's heavy. A typical sheet of ¾-in.-thick MDF weighs about 100 lb., so it's no fun hoisting it onto the table saw. It's also prone to water damage and doesn't hold screws and other fasteners well, especially in its edges.

Hardware

Most of these projects include hardware of some sort—ranging from screws or nails to hinges, drawer slides, and specialty items, like T-track for hold-downs and the like. You can find much of the hardware at your local home-supply store, and what you can't find there is available from mail-order wood-working-supply houses (see Sources on p. 172). In the cut lists included with most projects, I've listed a supplier and part number for any specialty hardware used.

I strongly recommend that you don't skimp on the quality of the hardware you use. Cheap drawer slides are available, for example, but they won't give you good service over the years. After all, you're putting a lot of work into a project. Why sully it with poorly made hinges, catches, and drawer slides that may give you problems before long?

Translating Cut Lists

CUT-LIST DIMENSIONS are listed in order of thickness, then width, then length. The length dimension always follows the grain dimension of lumber or the face grain of plywood. Although the pieces shown here are all the same size, their cut-list dimensions read differently.

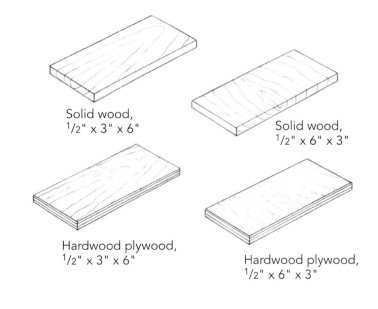

Solid wood,
1/2" x 3" x 6"

Solid wood,
1/2" x 6" x 3"

Hardwood plywood,
1/2" x 3" x 6"

Hardwood plywood,
1/2" x 6" x 3"

General Tips and Techniques

For each project, the chapter provides step-by-step instructions particular to that piece. However, I'll discuss here certain general woodworking procedures that apply to just about every project.

Reading cut lists

The dimensions in the cut lists are presented in order of thickness, then width, and then length. Note that the length dimension always follows the grain direction of lumber or the face grain of plywood (see the drawing "Translating Cut Lists" at left). Although finished sizes are given in the cut lists, it's best to take your workpiece measurement directly from an opening or frame when appropriate, such as when fitting backs, drawer bottoms, or inset doors and drawer fronts.

Laying out

The first step in any project is to lay out your lumber and sheet goods to rough size in preparation for milling to thickness. With lumber, I always begin with roughsawn boards, rather than prethicknessed stock. I use a stick of chalk to lay out the boards a few inches oversize in length and about 1/4 in. oversize in width. I crosscut and rip the boards to rough size, then mill them to final size (see the sidebar "Dressing Stock with Machines" on the facing page). I mill extra stock for tool setups at the same time, so I can be assured the test pieces will be the same dimensions as the project stock.

When laying out plywood, I inspect it first for flaws using a strong, glancing sidelight in a darkened shop (see photos L and M on the facing page). I sweep the light both along and across the grain. Remember that plywood often varies in thickness from piece to piece. Thus, dado joints and rabbet joints will fit better if all of the parts that slip into those joints are cut from the same piece of plywood.

DRESSING STOCK WITH MACHINES

To ensure accurate joinery and straight lines in your furniture, it's necessary to dress your stock flat, straight, and square. It's best to begin with oversize, roughsawn lumber because it's already done most of its warping during the drying process. Therefore, you'll be able to plane and joint it to final thickness and width with minimal warping. If you begin with warped premilled lumber, you can't flatten it without losing thickness. Here's a quick overview of proper stock dressing using machinery. You can also flatten and thickness stock with handplanes following the same basic sequence.

1. If your roughsawn stock is fairly bowed or cupped, begin by ripping and crosscutting it into smaller pieces. For safe ripping on the table saw, joint one edge of the stock straight for feeding against the rip fence. Allow a couple of extra inches in length and ¼ in. extra in width for each piece.

2. Flatten one face on the jointer. For stability, feed the stock with the concave face down. Cut with the slope of the grain to minimize tearout.

3. Plane the stock to final thickness, feeding it through a thickness planer, with the previously flattened side on the planer table. Cut with the slope of the grain.

4. Joint one edge of the thicknessed board square. Feed with the concave edge down.

5. Rip the piece to width on the table saw.

6. Crosscut one end square, measure for length, and then crosscut the opposite end to length.

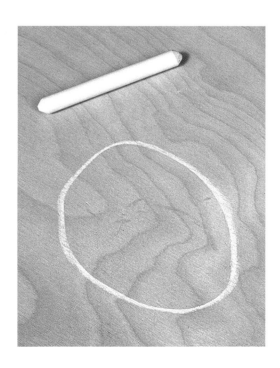
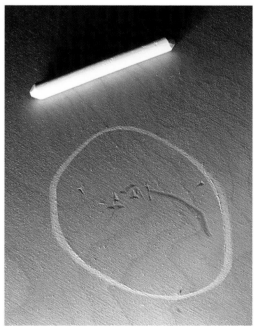

PHOTOS L AND M: Before laying out plywood, inspect it for flaws using a strong, glancing sidelight in a darkened shop. The scar circled in the left photo is barely visible in normal light, but under a sidelight (right photo), it's immediately apparent.

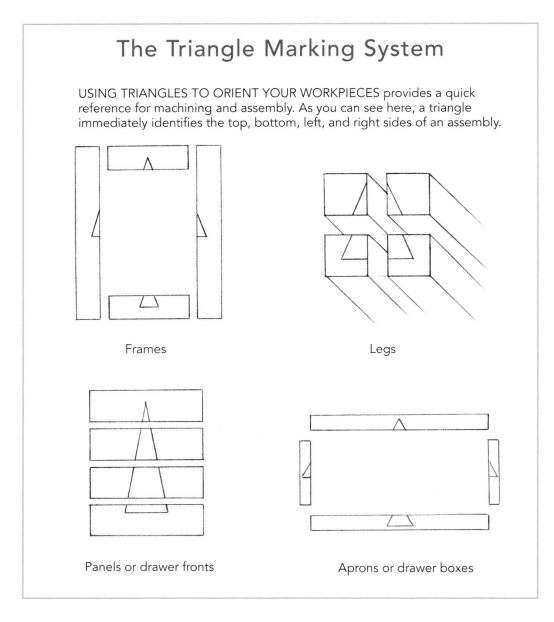

The Triangle Marking System

USING TRIANGLES TO ORIENT YOUR WORKPIECES provides a quick reference for machining and assembly. As you can see here, a triangle immediately identifies the top, bottom, left, and right sides of an assembly.

Frames

Legs

Panels or drawer fronts

Aprons or drawer boxes

For orienting individual parts, I use the triangle marking system, which tells me at a glance how a part relates to its mates (see the drawing "The Triangle Marking System" above).

Assembly Tips

+ Always do a dry clamp-up to rehearse your clamping procedures. While a cabinet is dry-clamped, fit its back snugly into its rabbets so you'll be able to insert it unglued to hold the case square while the glue cures.

+ I typically apply glue to both mating surfaces, except when applying solid-wood edging to plywood. For that, I just apply a thick coat to the plywood edge. An ink roller works well for spreading a thin, even coat of glue. For brushing glue onto tenons, tongues, and into mortises, I use a solder flux brush. A small artist's brush is good for getting into small holes and grooves.

+ When gluing up, work on a flat surface. If a piece isn't lying flat, you won't be able to accurately check it for square.

+ Use contact cement to attach thick leather pads to pipe-clamp jaws to prevent damage to workpieces.

- Use cauls to distribute clamping pressure, centering them over the joint. To span long joints, use crowned cauls (see the drawing "Clamping Cauls" below). On smaller pieces, it's easier to use cauls that almost cover the entire piece being clamped.
- If a piece isn't square under clamping pressure, try shifting the angle of the clamps on the joints to bring the piece into square.

- To clean up excess glue, use a clean rag and clean water, replenishing the water as necessary to prevent wiping diluted glue into wood grain and jeopardizing the finish. Alternatively, wait until the glue has cured to a rubbery consistency, then pare it away with a sharp chisel.

Clamping Cauls

CAULS DISTRIBUTE CLAMPING PRESSURE across joints. Make long cauls from thick hardwood. Cutting the ends squarely will aid in assembly when standing the cauls on end on the bench.

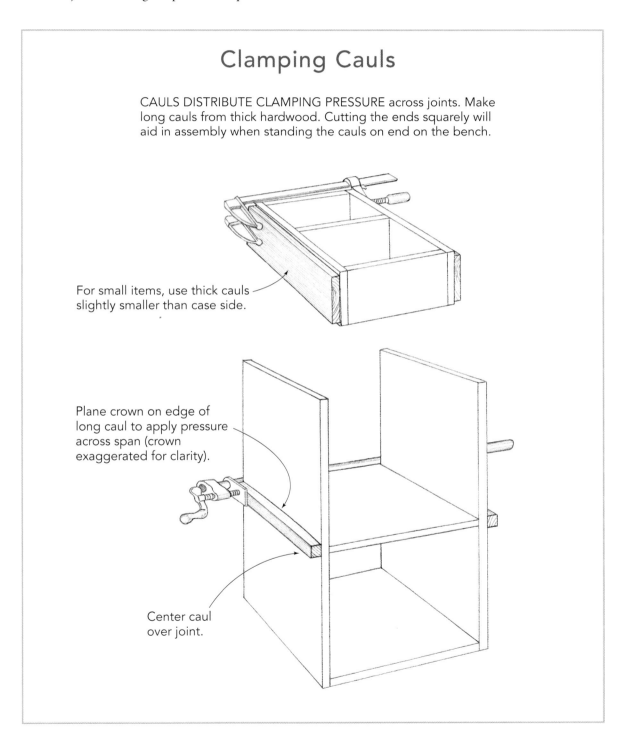

For small items, use thick cauls slightly smaller than case side.

Plane crown on edge of long caul to apply pressure across span (crown exaggerated for clarity).

Center caul over joint.

A clamp rack should keep all of your various clamps organized, visible, and accessible without wasting a lot of shop space.

CLAMP RACKS

I F THERE'S ONE THING that most woodworkers can't get enough of it's clamps. (Well, wood too. OK, and machines and jigs . . .) Unfortunately, clamps—particularly pipe and bar clamps—can take up a lot of space, and they need to be stored in some kind of organized fashion so you can quickly select the right clamps for the job at hand. Clamps dumped in boxes can be as aggravating to pick through as a jumble of wire coat hangers.

A clamp rack of some sort is usually the best solution, but it has to be strong; metal clamps are heavy. Racks can be designed as wall-hung, standing, or mobile units. The type of rack that will suit you best depends on your particular existing and future inventory of clamps. If your shop is small or if you have a single dedicated assembly area, wall-hung or standing racks might be fine. Just make sure that a standing unit either has a large enough footprint to prevent it from tipping or can be screwed to a wall. If, on the other hand, you tend to assemble projects in various areas of a larger shop, a mobile unit would probably be your best bet. In this chapter, we'll take a look at all of these options.

WALL RACK FOR PIPE AND BAR CLAMPS

Laying Out the Parts

1. If you'll be mounting to a wood-frame wall, begin by locating the appropriate wall studs. They will most likely be spaced 16 in. on center.

2. Determine the length of the rack by measuring from center to center between the outermost wall studs to which the rack will be attached. Add at least 2 in. to that length.

3. Lay out the backboard. Mark it with the locations of the wall-stud centerlines.

4. Lay out the dadoes to accept the brackets, staying at least 1 in. away from your stud centerlines for drill access later. To determine the spacing for each pair of brackets, I calculate the distance necessary to accommodate the pipes or bars, then add ³⁄₁₆ in. The spacing between the pairs is determined by the depth of your clamp jaws and the wall studs. If you want to be able to hang clamps with deeper jaws, space the pairs farther apart.

5. Using cardboard or scrap plywood, make a pattern of the bracket shape (see the drawing "Bracket Layout" on p. 20).

H ere's a simple rack you can make from plywood or particleboard. This stacking type of rack significantly reduces the amount of wall space needed for hanging clamps. The small "nose" of the gusset-shape brackets makes inserting clamps easier than if the brackets were square. I made this particular rack from scraps of ¾-in.-thick hardwood plywood and MDF. You could use construction plywood, but it often has voids that are liable to compromise strength in this situation. For joinery, shallow dadoes cut in the backboard align the pieces for assembly and provide a bit more glue surface to the joint. Once it's glued and screwed together, this rack is incredibly strong. I painted it so it wouldn't look scrappy.

Cutting the Parts and Joints

1. Rip the backboard to width. Using the same rip-fence setting, rip enough lengths of material to make the necessary number of brackets. Crosscut the backboard to length.

2. Using your pattern, lay out the brackets. To make the most economical use of your plywood, place angled edges adjacent to each other as shown in the drawing.

3. Saw the brackets to shape. After making your square crosscuts, you can cut the angled edge with a bandsaw or jigsaw and then clean up the cut with a belt or disk sander. Alternatively, you can outfit a table-saw

Wall Rack for Pipe and Bar Clamps

Screw,
#8 x 2$^{1}/_{2}$"

Backboard

Space dadoes to suit pipe or bar width.

Dado, $^{1}/_{8}$" x $^{3}/_{4}$"

Bracket

TIP

It's best to mount any hanging clamp rack so that its ends terminate near wall studs. Otherwise, the weight of the clamps can pull the unsupported section away from the wall.

PHOTO A: To get a straight, clean cut on the bracket's angled edge, you can outfit a table-saw crosscut sled with two fences set at 90 degrees to each other and at 45 degrees to the line of cut.

When attaching pieces with both glue and screws, I first drill any pilot holes or clearance holes with the pieces dry-clamped together. Drilling after applying glue can gum up your bit.

crosscut sled with two fences set at 45 degrees to the blade path (see photo on p. 19).

4. Saw or rout the ⅛-in.-deep dadoes, aiming for a snug fit to accept the brackets.

Assembling and Mounting the Rack

1. Temporarily clamp the brackets into their dadoes and predrill (no more than 3 in. apart) for 2½-in.-long drywall screws. Drill a

pilot hole to prevent splitting the brackets. Also drill a screw-clearance hole through the backboard to allow the pieces to pull tightly together.

2. Apply a liberal amount of glue to the rear edge of each bracket and to the dado. Screw the brackets firmly in place.

3. After the glue dries, paint the rack if you like, then mount it to the wall using long screws. If mounting to a concrete or brick wall, use self-tapping concrete screws or lag screws and anchors.

A RACK FOR F-STYLE BAR CLAMPS

Small, quick-set bar clamps, also referred to as F-style clamps, are best hung on a rack similar to Tony O'Malley's unit shown here. The rack consists of two parallel boards set into case sides that angle outward toward the bottom. The clamp head hooks on the upper board, while the lower board keeps the clamp body from swinging. The slope of the unit tends to keep the clamp's bar pressed against both boards. A screw cleat that attaches to the case sides in back allows fastening the unit to the wall.

Bracket Layout

WALL RACK FOR PARALLEL-JAW CLAMPS

MORE AND MORE woodworkers these days are discovering parallel-jaw clamps. The boxlike jaws on these heavy-duty clamps are deep, and they close parallel to each other, making them useful for assembly work. If you're a fan of these clamps, as is woodworker Walt Segl, you may want to build this rack that he designed specifically to provide compact, accessible storage for his collection. The rack is simple to make. Its construction is similar to the previous wall rack for pipe and bar clamps, except this one is made entirely from ¾-in.-thick solid wood. Segl used cherry, but any hardwood will do.

Making the Rack

1. Determine the length of the backboard. If you'll be mounting the rack on a wood-frame wall, make sure the ends of the rack terminate over wall studs, as explained in the previous wall-rack project.

Wall Rack for Parallel-Jaw Clamps

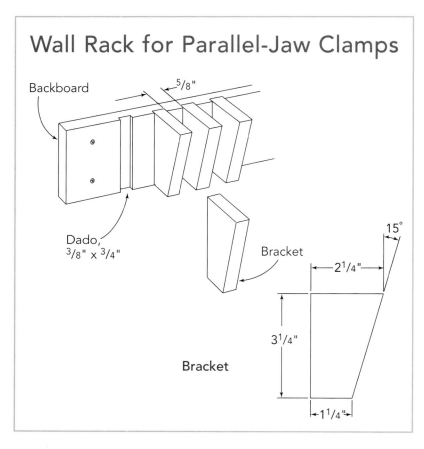

Backboard

5/8"

Dado,
3/8" x 3/4"

Bracket

Bracket

15°

2 1/4"

3 1/4"

1 1/4"

2. Mill the stock for the backboard and the brackets, ripping it into strips about 3¼ in. wide.

3. Mark the stud spacing on the backboard. Lay out the ⅜-in.-deep dadoes, spacing them ⅝ in. apart. Make sure no dado lies on a stud-center location. Rather than laying out all the dadoes, you can simply calculate the locations of the first and last slot and then saw the dadoes as described in step 5.

4. Crosscut the brackets from the length of stock you prepared. To avoid constant reset-ting, it's easier to use two saws: one for mak-ing the square cut and one set to 15 degrees for making the angled cut (see the drawing "Wall Rack for Parallel-Jaw Clamps" at left). A table saw and a chopsaw work well in tandem for this.

5. Rout or saw the dadoes in the backboard. If you have a good dado head, the easiest approach is to cut them on the table saw using an indexing pin on a miter-gauge aux-iliary fence (see the drawing "Cutting the

Cutting the Backboard Dadoes

A QUICK WAY TO CUT A SERIES OF EVENLY SPACED DADOES is to use an indexing pin set into an auxiliary miter-gauge fence. After cutting the first dado without the auxil-iary fence and pin, clamp or screw the fence to the miter gauge and adjust it so the pin is ⅝'' away from the blade, then cut the dadoes as shown.

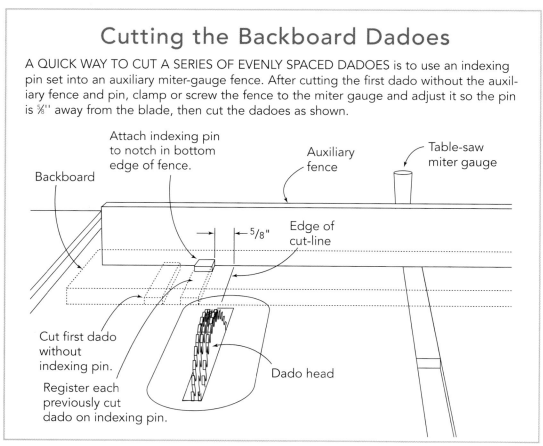

Attach indexing pin to notch in bottom edge of fence.

Auxiliary fence

Table-saw miter gauge

Backboard

5/8"

Edge of cut-line

Cut first dado without indexing pin.

Register each previously cut dado on indexing pin.

Dado head

A CHIN-UP BAR FOR CLAMPS

Mike Callihan cobbled together this simple rack to carry his parallel-jaw and F-style bar clamps. He simply attached several brackets to a cleat board, then slipped a long pipe through holes drilled in the cleats. The clamp handles slip over the metal pipe, which is able to carry the considerable weight of all these clamps. For strength, he used bolts rather than screws to fasten the rack to his wall.

Backboard Dadoes" on facing page). This allows you to quickly cut slot after slot without measuring. Aim for a snug fit with the brackets.

6. Dry-assemble the brackets into their slots to make sure everything fits well. To make clamping easier, bevel-rip a 2x4 at 15 degrees for use as a clamping caul (see the drawing "Beveled Clamping" at right).

7. Apply a thick coat of glue to the rear edge of each bracket and a thinner coat into each dado. Make sure that the top edges of all the parts are lined up well. Clamp the brackets into their dadoes.

8. Mount the rack on the wall using long screws.

Beveled Clamping Caul

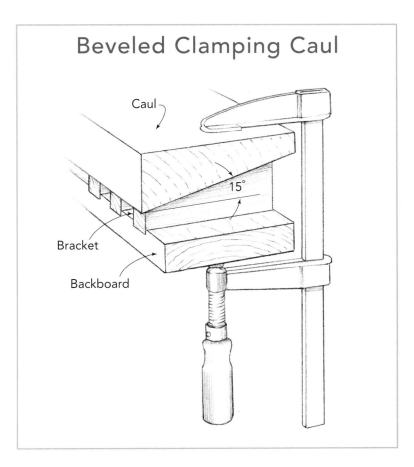

Caul

15°

Bracket

Backboard

CLAMP CABINET

Craig Bentzley has a lot of different types of clamps, and he decided to build a clamp cabinet to accommodate them all. The cabinet is built from inexpensive pine boards, wooden closet pole rods, and commonly available hardware. Bentzley dressed up the cabinet with simple moldings, a few corbels, and gave the whole unit a coat of paint. Too nice for a clamp cabinet? "Hey, I'm going to have to look at it for a long time," he says with no regrets.

This particular cabinet is the perfect size for Bentzley's needs. Yours, of course, will probably be different. No matter. Simply adjust the height and width to suit your shop space and clamp collection (see the drawings "Clamp Cabinet" on facing page and "Shelf and Dowel Spacing" on p. 26). However, you'll probably want to keep the depth of the cabinet similar for clamp accessibility.

This cabinet includes shelves to store belt clamps, pipe connectors, extra pipe-clamp heads, etc. (see photo B on p. 27). Wooden rails and an aluminum angle fastened to the wall at the rear provide purchase for spring clamps of different sizes. The top of Bentzley's cabinet is home to a bevy of handscrews.

Making the cabinet is a simple matter of sawing the parts to size, cutting a few joints, and assembling the pieces with glue, nails, and screws. After assembling the case, you'll fit the shelves and dowel rods into place.

Clamp Cabinet

THIS CABINET, CONSTRUCTED OF SOLID PINE, is put together with simple joints. The bottom is nailed and glued into a rabbet in each side. The dividers sit in dadoes in the bottom, and the top is screwed to the vertical members. The corbels are attached with glue and biscuits, and the bottom rail and molding is simply nailed in place.

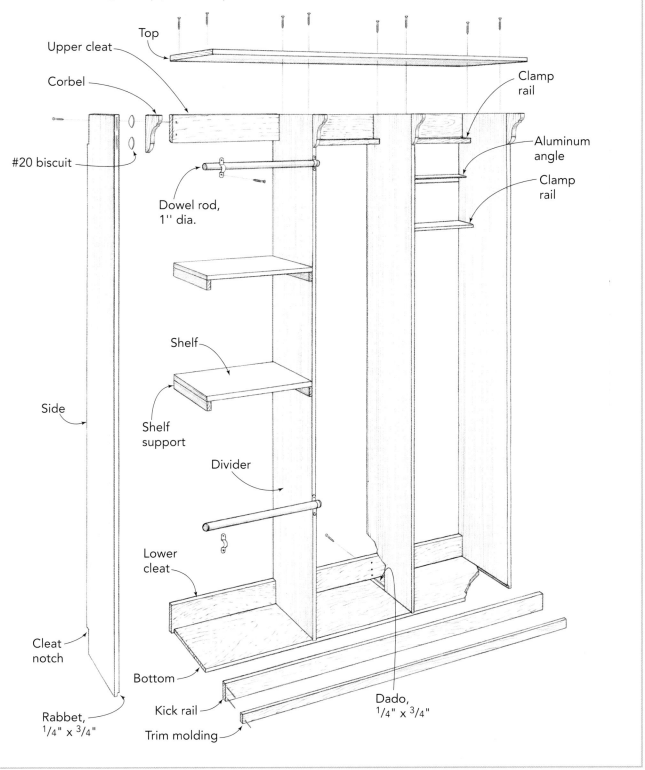

Top

Upper cleat

Corbel

Clamp rail

#20 biscuit

Aluminum angle

Clamp rail

Dowel rod, 1'' dia.

Shelf

Side

Shelf support

Divider

Lower cleat

Cleat notch

Bottom

Dado, $^1/_4$" x $^3/_4$"

Rabbet, $^1/_4$" x $^3/_4$"

Kick rail

Trim molding

Shelf and Dowel Spacing

FOR YOUR REFERENCE, this drawing shows the overall dimensions, compartment sizes, and dowel spacing that worked for the designer. You may want to adjust the spacing to suit your own clamp collection.

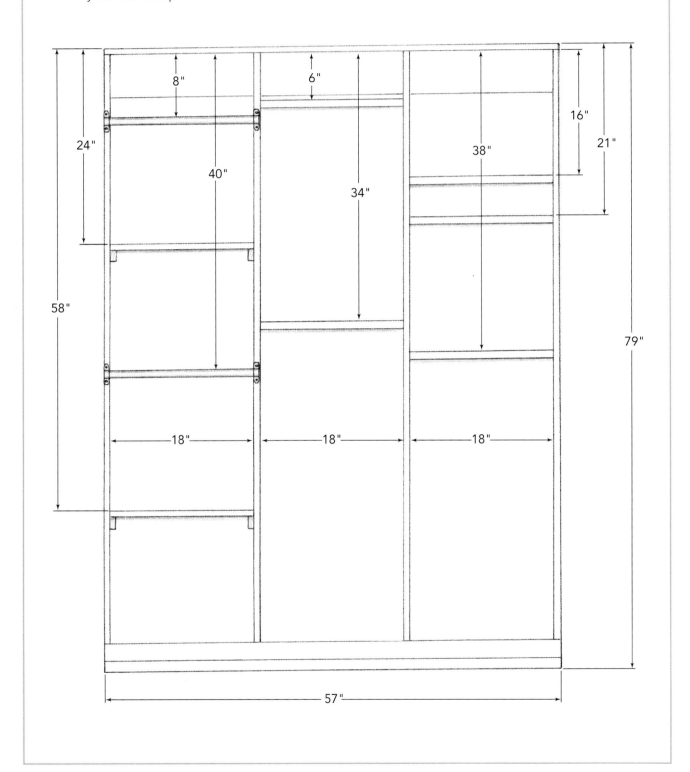

CUT LIST FOR CLAMP CABINET

4	Sides and dividers	¾" x 7¼" x 79"	Solid wood or plywood
1	Top	¾" x 11¼" x 57"	Solid wood or plywood
1	Bottom	¾" x 6½" x 56"	Solid wood or plywood
1	Upper cleat	¾" x 5½" x 57"	Solid wood
1	Lower cleat	¾" x 4½" x 57"	Solid wood
4	Corbels	¾" x 3½" x 4¾"	Solid wood
1	Kick rail	¾" x 3½" x 57"	Solid wood
1	Trim molding	⅜" x 1⅜" x 57"	Solid wood
2	Shelves	¾" x 8½" x 18"	Solid wood or plywood
4	Shelf supports	¾" x 1½" x 7¼"	Solid wood
1	Clamp rail	¾" x 1½" x 18"	Solid wood
2	Clamp rails	¼" x 2½" x 18"	Solid wood
2	Dowel rods	1" dia. x 19½"	
5	Dowel rods	1" dia. x 17⅞"	
1	Aluminum angle	1¼" x 1¼"	

TIP

Manila file folders make great pattern material. The stiff paper cuts easily but is thick enough to serve as a pencil guide for tracing outlines.

Making the Parts

1. Begin by making a pattern of the corbel from cardboard or stiff paper (see the drawing "Corbel Pattern" on p. 28).

2. Rip and crosscut all of the parts to size. Rip the shelves to width (front to back), but leave them slightly oversize in length for now. You'll cut them to fit snugly between the dividers after assembly.

3. Prepare a single 3½-in.-wide board that's long enough for all of the corbels, but don't crosscut it into individual corbel blanks yet. It's much easier to cut biscuit slots in a long board than in short pieces.

PHOTO B: Various commercial brackets are available for hanging dowel rods. Shelves provide a resting place for items like pipe connectors and belt clamps that are difficult to hang.

4. Lay out the corbels on the board. Mark and cut two #20 biscuit slots in each corbel. Crosscut the individual corbel blanks from the board, and cut the mating slots for each one in the cabinet sides and dividers.

5. Cut the corbels to shape using a scrollsaw or jigsaw. A bandsaw will work, but the saw marks will be difficult to clean up in the stepped areas. Set the shaped corbels aside for now.

6. If you like, rout a decorative edge on the trim molding. Bentzley used a scrap piece of ogee molding he had lying around.

Cutting the Joints

1. Cut the rabbets in the lower ends of the sides. You can either rout these or cut them on the table saw using a dado head (see photo C on facing page).

TIP

If you're not going to paint the cabinet and prefer that the cleat ends don't show, forgo cutting the notches. Instead, cut the cleats to butt against the inside faces of the sides. You can nail or screw through the sides and into the ends of the cleats during assembly.

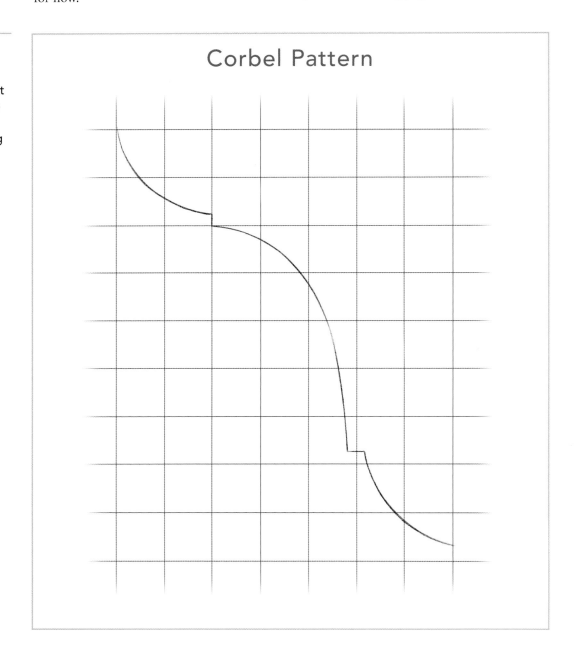

Corbel Pattern

PHOTO C: One way to easily cut rabbets in the ends of long boards is to use a cross-cut sled to feed the workpiece across a dado head on the table saw.

2. Cut the dadoes in the bottom to accept the dividers. Again, you can rout these or cut them with a dado head on the table saw.

3. Lay out and cut the notches in the ends of the sides and dividers to accept the upper and lower cleats. Remember that the lower notches on the dividers will be ½ in. shorter than those on the sides because of the dadoes in the cabinet bottom.

Assembling the Case

The case is easy to assemble because only the corbels have to be clamped in place. The rest of the joints are held with nails or screws.

1. Using biscuits, glue the corbels to the sides and dividers (see photo D on p. 30). After the glue dries, sand the joint flush.

2. Dry-assemble the whole case to make sure that all the joints fit well and that all of the pieces line up properly. Using a square, mark the location of the dividers across the back face of the upper cleat. Glue and screw the bottom to the dividers.

3. In preparation for attaching the sides and cleats, lay the assembly face down on the floor, straddling a couple of 4x4s to protect the corbels. Use glue and finish nails to attach the sides to the bottom. Make sure the bottom is pulled up snugly into its rabbet.

4. Square up the case by comparing its diagonal measurements. Glue and screw the upper cleat into its notches. Use the marks you made on the back of the cleat to line up the dividers. Attach the lower cleat.

5. Glue and screw the ¼-in.-thick clamp rails to the underside of the upper cleat. Screw the top to the case.

TIP

When ripping plywood into pieces, plan your cut sequence so that all factory edges are cut away in the process, leaving clean-cut edges.

PHOTO D: After cutting the biscuit joints, clamp the corbels in place using clamps with soft jaw pads.

6. Screw the shelf supports in place. Don't glue them, in case you want to move them at some point. Trim the shelves for a snug fit in their openings, and nail them to their supports.

7. Glue and nail the kick rail in place. Tack on the trim molding.

8. All that's left to do is to install the various dowel rods and clamp rails. Check your local home- and building-supply outlets for rod brackets and aluminum angles. To hold his spring clamps, Bentzley attached the aluminum angle and clamp rail to the wall studs

(see the photo on p. 16). If that doesn't work for you, however, you can attach the pieces by fastening the ends to the case sides.

Finishing Up

If you're going to paint the unit, it's usually easiest to do so before installing it. Afterward, mount it to the wall, screwing through the upper and lower cleats into the wall studs.

MOBILE CLAMP RACK

F YOU FIND THAT you're often lugging a lot of clamps to various assembly areas, a mobile clamp rack might be just the thing for you. Bill Hylton designed this portable unit for use at his various assembly stations. The rack, made from plywood and some solid-wood strips, is strong enough to carry hundreds of pounds of clamps. It's also stable because of its wide footprint and its A-frame shape, which prevent the rack from being top heavy.

The rack will accommodate all sorts of clamps. Of course, you can adjust the dimensions of the rack to suit your clamp collection and shop space. One nice feature of this unit is the handscrew compartment, which includes a ramp to keep handscrews from vibrating off the rack. A short 2x4 post between the jaws keeps the clamps aligned on top of each other. Both faces of the rack are constructed in the same fashion, although the spacing varies to accommodate different clamps (see drawing "Elevations" on p. 34).

Making the Parts

1. Begin by crosscutting a sheet of 48-in.-wide plywood to 52 in. long. You can do this accurately with a portable circular saw and guide (see photo E on p. 33). Lay out and cut the sheet into halves as shown in step 1 of the drawing "Cutting the Sides and Dividers" on page 35.

2. Saw or rout a dado and rabbet into each half as shown in step 2 of the drawing. To cut the dado, register the router fence or rip fence against the long, straight edge of the panel.

3. Lay out a divider on each half, as shown in step 3 of the drawing. Saw off the divider, again using a portable circular saw and guide.

Mobile Clamp Rack

THIS RACK IS MADE FROM ¾''-thick hardwood plywood, glued and screwed together. The solid-wood clamp support rails are screwed to the divider and case sides. Twin rails help keep longer clamps from swinging freely. Space the rails to suit your collection of clamps. A ramped shelf and center post keep handscrews from wandering around.

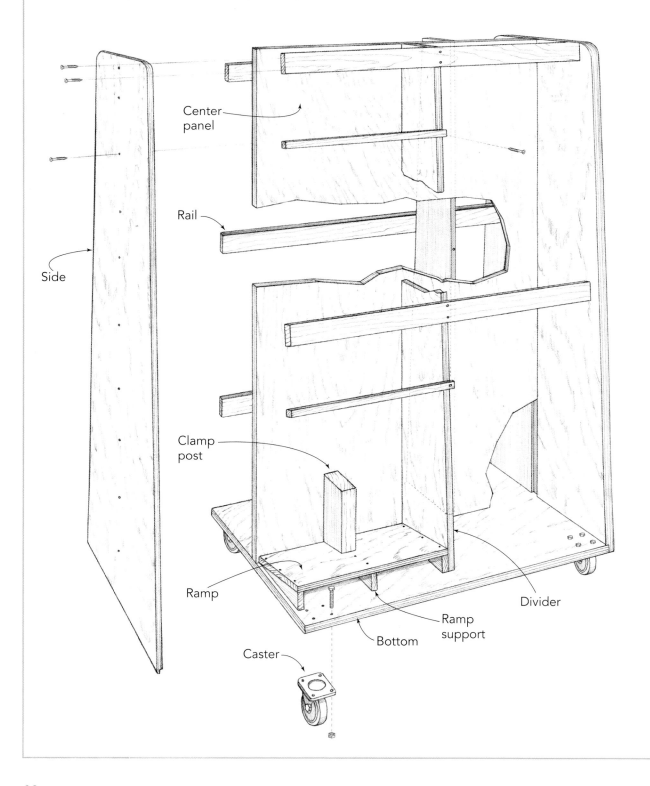

Center panel

Side

Rail

Clamp post

Ramp

Caster

Bottom

Ramp support

Divider

PHOTO E: This guide for cutting sheet goods is made from two pieces of straight-edged plywood. The lower piece is attached oversize, then trimmed off by the saw running against the upper fence piece. The resulting cut edge can then be clamped directly against the cut line.

4. Trim off the rabbet from the end of each divider piece. The sides and dividers are now complete.

5. Saw the bottom and center panel to size.

6. Mill the rails but leave them slightly oversize in length for now, as you'll want to fit them snugly between the sides after assembling the case.

7. Saw the ramp and supports. The wedge-shaped supports can be safely cut to shape using a bandsaw or jigsaw. Cut the clamp post to size.

Assembling the Rack

1. Lightly mark a vertical centerline on the outside face of each side and on the underside of the bottom.

2. Using a ⁹⁄₆₄-in.-dia. bit, drill the screw-clearance holes in the sides and bottom to allow the pieces to pull together tightly. Counterbore the holes in the sides if you plan to plug the holes as Hylton did.

3. Clamping across the top and bottom of the case, dry-assemble the center panel, sides,

CUT LIST FOR MOBILE CLAMP RACK			
1	Panel for sides and dividers	¾" x 48" x 52"	Hardwood plywood
1	Center panel	¾" x 35" x 51¼"	Hardwood plywood
1	Bottom	¾" x 24" x 35"	Hardwood plywood
1	Ramp	¾" x 8½" x 17⅞"	Hardwood plywood
3	Ramp supports	¾" x 2" x 8½"	Hardwood plywood
2	Rails	¾" x 2½" x 34½"	Solid wood
3	Rails	¾" x 2" x 34½"	Solid wood
2	Rails	¾" x 1" x 18⅝"	Solid wood
1	Rail	¾" x 1" x 12"	Solid wood
1	Clamp post	1½" x 3½" x 12"	Solid wood

and bottom together to make sure all the parts line up well and to rehearse your clamp-up procedures.

4. Remove the bottom clamp and the rack bottom. Temporarily attach the sides to the center panel using one screw through each side near the bottom. Apply a thick bead of glue to the bottom edge of the center panel and attach the bottom, screwing it to the center panel with 2-in.-long drywall screws (see photo F on facing page).

5. Remove the sides. Glue and screw them to the bottom and center panel.

6. Glue and screw the dividers in place. Spacers placed against each side will help

hold the dividers in place for attachment (see photo G on facing page).

7. Screw the ramp supports in place. Attach the ramp and clamp support post.

8. Trim the rails for a snug fit between the sides, and screw them into place. Don't glue them, in case you decide at some point to rearrange their spacing. Attach the rails to the dividers first, then to the sides. Spacer blocks clamped to the sides will help hold the ends of the rails in position for attachment.

9. Attach heavy-duty casters, as they will have to carry a lot of weight.

Elevations

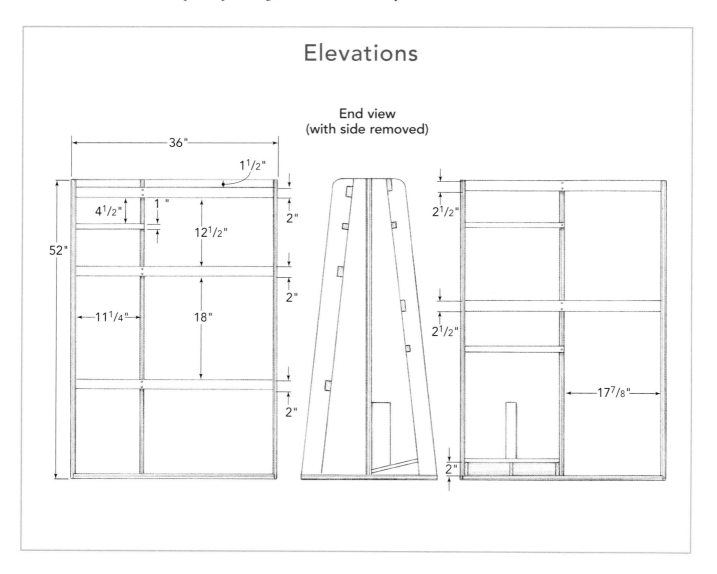

End view
(with side removed)

Cutting the Sides and Dividers

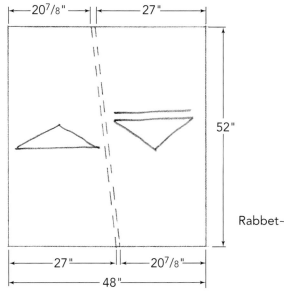

1. Cut plywood as shown (each half will yield one rack side and one divider).

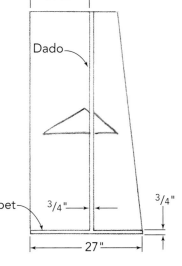

2. In each half, saw or rout ¼" x ¾" dado and rabbet.

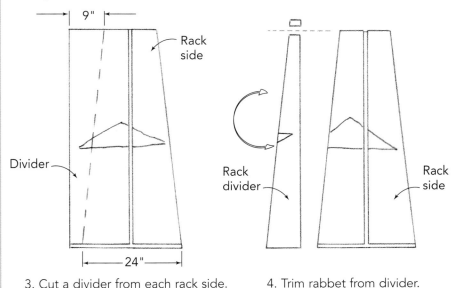

3. Cut a divider from each rack side.

4. Trim rabbet from divider.

Finishing Up

1. If you counterbored holes in the side, make plugs and glue them into their holes. After the glue dries, pare and sand the plugs flush to the plywood.

2. Using 150-grit sandpaper, slightly round all of the edges.

3. If you like, you can apply a couple of coats of finish after a light sanding.

PHOTO F: After temporarily attaching the sides to the center panel with one screw each, glue the bottom panel to the center panel.

PHOTO G: When attaching the dividers, use spacers to temporarily hold them in position for screwing.

Well-designed lumber racks are sturdy and provide easy access for picking through your stash of boards and hard-to-throw-away offcuts.

WOOD RACKS

OF ALL THE ITEMS IN A SHOP, wood is among the most space hungry. Lumber and sheet goods range in size from long boards and full sheets to diminutive offcuts of exotic wood too precious to pitch. It all needs a place to live where you can get to it easily when you need it.

It can be backbreaking work to sort through the boards lying on the floor, and it subjects them to moisture. Standing boards on end against a wall requires a tall ceiling. The most practical solution for most shops is storing boards on racks where they can be organized into accessible piles by species. Although racks can be any size, a good rule of thumb is that any lumber rack should minimally accommodate 8-ft.-long boards. Ideally, you'll also want storage for boards up to16 ft., which aren't uncommon. (You don't want to crosscut long boards just to store them because leaving them long allows you to maximize stock when laying out a project.)

A typical lumber rack incorporates cantilevered arms, which allow easy access to boards. For strength, use hardwood or thick construction lumber for long arms that will support a lot of boards. When determining the vertical spacing of the arms, you'll need to strike a balance between storage capacity and accessibility. Spacing them farther apart provides greater capacity but hinders access to the bottom boards, while closer spacing (and more arms) costs room overall but increases accessibility. It's important that boards lie flat and straight. Therefore, rows of arms must be installed along the same plane, and freestanding racks may need leveling on uneven floors.

As for sheet goods, unless you have a production cabinet shop, you probably don't keep a large inventory of plywood, particleboard, and other man-made boards. You may need only enough space to store a dozen or so full-size sheets as well as their inevitable offcuts. In this chapter, you'll find several solutions to suit your needs.

WALL-MOUNTED LUMBER RACK

WHEN BILL HYLTON designed his lumber racks, he decided that he wanted lots of storage for long boards as well as usable offcuts (see the photo on p. 36). His wall-mounted system incorporates columns with cantilevered arms for the long boards, and a lower section for piles of offcuts up to 2 ft. long.

The columns that make up the rack consist of recycled 2x4 construction lumber sandwiched between lengths of ¾-in. by 3-in.-thick pine. The cantilevered arms are bolted to the columns and bolstered by ¾-in.-thick plywood gussets, which add bearing strength. Most of the arms are 16 in. long. The uppermost arms are 24 in. long to provide easier access to the top row. Screw blocks placed intermittently in the column allow attachment to wall studs. The columns are spaced 32 in. apart horizontally— lag-screwed to every other wall stud. The top end of each column is fastened above to a shimmed-out floor joist to reduce strain on the wall. (If your floor joists run perpendicular to the wall, you can attach a board to them in front of the columns for reinforcement.)

The lower section of each column assembly consists of a 24-in.-high by 24-in.-deep frame. The frame rails are the same thickness as the arms and are sandwiched between the column members and the front legs. Plywood nailed to the top of each frame helps keep the rails solidly in place.

Making the Parts

1. Calculate how many columns you'll need to suit your available space, then decide how many arms you'll want. Make a cut list of all the parts you'll need. The sizes of the individual parts are listed on the drawing "Wall-Mounted Lumber Rack" on the facing page.

Wall-Mounted Lumber Rack

EACH COLUMN ASSEMBLY consists of arms, rails, and screw blocks sandwiched between the column uprights and legs. Plywood gussets add bearing strength to the arms. A plywood platform sits atop the upper rails to create storage area underneath for short pieces of stock.

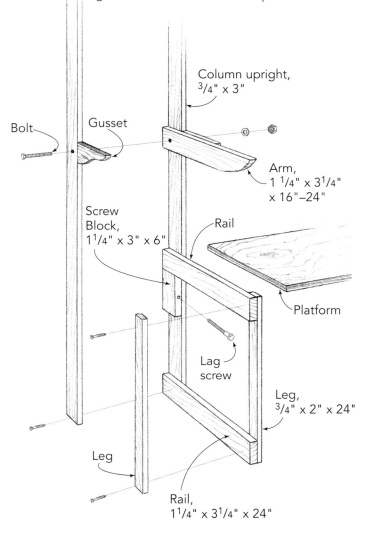

Column upright,
3/4" x 3"

Bolt

Gusset

Arm,
1 1/4" x 3 1/4"
x 16"–24"

Screw
Block,
1 1/4" x 3" x 6"

Rail

Platform

Lag
screw

Leg,
3/4" x 2" x 24"

Leg

Rail,
1 1/4" x 3 1/4" x 24"

TIP

Lumber racks provide the perfect opportunity to use recycled construction lumber. A few passes through the planer will clean it up nicely. Just make sure to first scrutinize boards for nails and other hardware.

Gusset Template

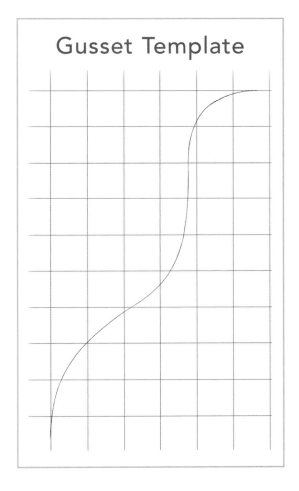

2. Cut the pieces to size. For the most secure fit, plane all of the arms, the screw blocks, and the rails to the same thickness. Shape the gussets and arms on the bandsaw (see the drawing "Gusset Template" above right). For the sake of efficiency, gang-saw the gussets (see photo A on p. 40).

3. Drill a ¾-in.-dia. by 1-in.-deep counter-bore in the center of each screw block. Drill a ⅜-in.-dia. hole through the block. This is best done on the drill press.

PHOTO A: When making the gussets, it's efficient to tape a stack of blanks together and gang-saw them on the bandsaw.

Assembling and Installing the Columns

1. Lay the column pieces side by side on the floor, and use a square to mark the location of the top edge of each row of arms, as well as the location of each upper rail.

2. Screw the columns together, sandwiching the screw blocks and rails between the vertical members. Screw the front legs to the ends of the rails.

3. Attach the column assemblies to the wall studs through the screw blocks using ⅜-in. by 4-in. lag screws with washers.

4. Glue and screw the gussets to the arms. Make sure that the rear edges of each pair of gussets are 3 in. from the end of the arm and parallel to each other.

5. Install the arms. Line up each arm to its mark, holding the gussets firmly against the column. Drill a ⅜-in.-dia. hole completely through the column and arm. Install a ⅜-in. by 3½-in. bolt with washer and nut to hold the arm in place.

FLOOR-TO-CEILING LUMBER RACKS

When Mike Callihan built his new shop, he dedicated a full room to lumber storage, running the lumber-rack posts from floor to ceiling. Each post is built up from five 2x6s of construction lumber, with the rack's arms sandwiched in between the pieces and projecting from both sides of the post. He connected the tops of each post to a 2x6 that spans the ceiling joists. The bottom of each post was likewise nailed to a length of 2x6 that is attached to the floor using concrete nails. These bottom 2x6s also serve as support for lumber to keep it off the concrete floor.

MODULAR FREESTANDING RACKS

DESIGNED THESE modular freestanding racks to hold both lumber and plywood. You can place the racks anywhere without tying them into your shop structure. Because the racks are modular, you can make as many as you like to hold whatever lengths of lumber you commonly use. The 7½-in.-wide center section accommodates sheet goods.

I made each of these separate modules about 6 ft. high, with the arms on each module spaced 2 ft. apart. I then spaced the modules 2 ft. from each other. You can store lumber on both sides of the rack. Even if one side is placed against a wall, you can still put long boards on that side, sliding them in and out from the end. To provide a platform for smooth insertion of boards onto the back arms, simply tack a length of ¼-in.-thick plywood across the arms.

The arms on these racks extend 12 in., although you could make them longer if you like. Using hardwood plywood for the arms is economical, and it's amazing how much weight they hold when glued and screwed to their posts. I made the posts from 6/4 poplar. If you decide to use construction-grade 2x4s instead, make sure they're straight and dry or your racks may eventually tweak out of shape as an earlier set of mine did.

Although you could simply shim under the feet of the modules to level them on an uneven floor, I installed lag screws in the feet, which allows for perfect adjustment.

If you have scrap plywood lying around, this is a good use for it. If you're using full sheets of plywood, the sizes given in the cut list will maximize the use of each sheet. For example, the ⅛-in.-wide saw kerf added to the width of a 3⅞-in. arm makes 4 in.—an even increment across the width of a 48-in.-wide sheet.

Modular Freestanding Racks

THIS MODULE IS MADE ALMOST ENTIRELY from hardwood plywood, with the exception of the posts and foot blocks. The end panels, arms, and feet are glued and screwed to the posts. The side panels are simply screwed on. Lag screws in the foot blocks allow for leveling the racks.

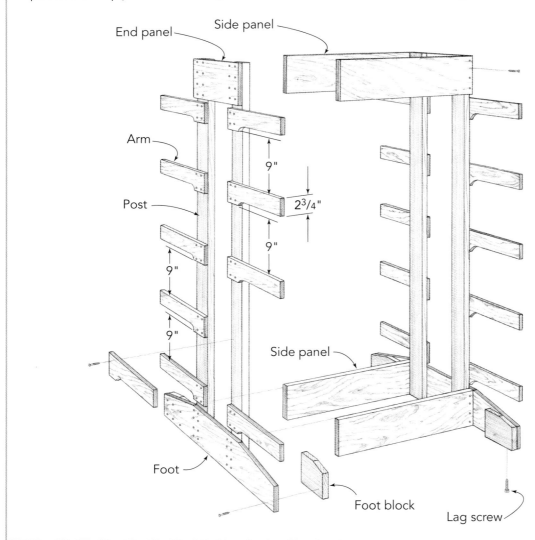

CUT LIST FOR MODULAR RACKS (FOR TWO MODULES)			
8	Posts	1½" x 3½" x 72"	Solid wood
40	Arms	¾" x 3⅞" x 15¾"	Hardwood plywood
4	Side panels	¾" x 7¼" x 23⅞"	Hardwood plywood
4	Side panels	¾" x 7⅞" x 22⅜"	Hardwood plywood
4	End panels	¾" x 7¼" x 14½"	Hardwood plywood
4	Feet	¾" x 7⅞" x 40"	Hardwood plywood
8	Foot blocks	1" x 5" x 7"	Solid wood

Making the Parts

1. Make the posts. If you're using construction lumber, it's good to plane, joint, or sand the outer faces to ensure a good glue bond with the arms.

2. Cut out the panels, the feet, and the blanks for the arms.

3. Shape the arms with a bandsaw or jigsaw. The cutaway on the underside allows more stacking room.

STORING VENEER AND DOWELS

In addition to boards, wood also comes in the form of dowels and veneer, of course. Veneer must be stored flat because it will buckle if stored on edge. Dowels are problematic thanks to their tendency to roll off shelves or lumber-rack arms. Craig Bentzley came up with a nice solution for dealing with both of these problems. Taking advantage of the light weight of veneer and dowels, he made racks to hang these materials from his shop ceiling, where they're accessible but out of the way.

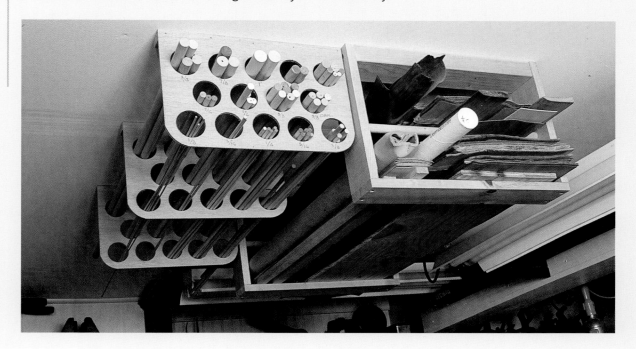

Assembling the Racks

1. Lay the posts side by side and mark out the arm spacing using a framing square.

2. Build the end assemblies, gluing and screwing the end panel and foot to each pair of posts.

3. Screw the side panels to the end assemblies. I don't glue these because I've occasionally needed to detach the end assemblies for moving or temporary storage.

4. If your floor isn't flat (mine sure isn't), make foot blocks to accept lag screws for leveling. Place each block in its position, and trace the slope of the plywood foot onto it.

5. Cut the sloped edge with the bandsaw or jigsaw. Glue and screw the blocks to the feet.

6. Drill pilot holes for the ½-in. by 3½-in. lag screws. To keep the holes square to the bottom of the feet, I used a jig that I predrilled on the drill press (see photo B). The flat on the top edge of the block allows you to clamp the jig to the foot.

7. Level the racks and load 'em up.

PHOTO B: A simple drilling jig clamped to the foot keeps the lag-screw holes square to the block.

THREE ALTERNATIVES FOR SHEET-GOODS STORAGE

Ideally, sheet goods should be stored flat to keep them that way, but many small shops can't afford the space. The best alternative is to stand the sheets up against a wall or in a rack. If you've got ceilings that are high enough, standing the sheets on their 4-ft. edge will save you some floor space. Ken Burton's vertical sheet-goods rack, built from construction lumber, includes interior compartments for small panels and offcuts. The bottom consists of 2x4s on edge that provide a platform to keep the sheets off the floor (see the photo below left).

A mobile plywood rack can be a good solution for a cramped shop or for situations where you want to wheel a lot of sheets to the table saw. Larry Seachrist used construction lumber to cobble together an A-frame rack that includes interior storage for long boards (see the photo below center).

If you're really pressed for shop space, consider attaching a plywood cabinet to the outside of your shop building, as Fred Matlack did. Constructing the cabinet at waist height makes grabbing the plywood so easy that even your teenage son or daughter won't mind helping you carry it into the shop (see the photo below right).

PLYWOOD RACK

ill Hylton's plywood rack stores a raft of panels and panel offcuts. Because the rack holds the panels at waist height, they're easier to lift and carry to the saw than panels resting on the floor. The top section of the rack leans back a bit to prevent panels from falling. The area behind is great for storing panel offcuts, and long, narrow pieces can be placed on top. The space underneath is ideal for lumber shorts or even for temporary housing of rolling carts. The unit—made from construction lumber and plywood—is relatively inexpensive to build. To create better joints, flatter surfaces, and a cleaner look, Hylton planed, jointed, and ripped his 2x4 lumber down to 1¼ in. by 3¼ in. You can skip this step if you like, but remember to adjust the lengths of the stiles and rails accordingly.

Making the Parts

1. Make the stiles and rails for the frames. Glue and screw the pieces together to make the four bottom frames. Make sure the frames are square.

2. Saw the uprights and beams to size. Glue and screw the uprights to the frames, making sure they're square to each other and that each upright sits 4 in. from the bottom of the frame as shown in the drawing "Plywood Rack (End View)" on p. 47.

3. Screw each beam between its pair of uprights, making sure they're square to each other.

4. Cut the braces. The easiest and most economical way to do this is to lay out the braces on a 32⅞-in. by 55¼-in. sheet of ¾-in.-thick plywood, as shown in the drawing "Brace Layout" on p. 47. Using a portable circular saw guided by a long, straight-edged piece of wood, trim off the first brace (see photo C on p. 47). The next brace can be ripped off using the table saw. Follow the same sequence to cut the rest.

Plywood Rack

THIS RACK IS MADE OF construction lumber and plywood. After gluing and screwing together the individual sections, they're connected by attaching the trough and top.

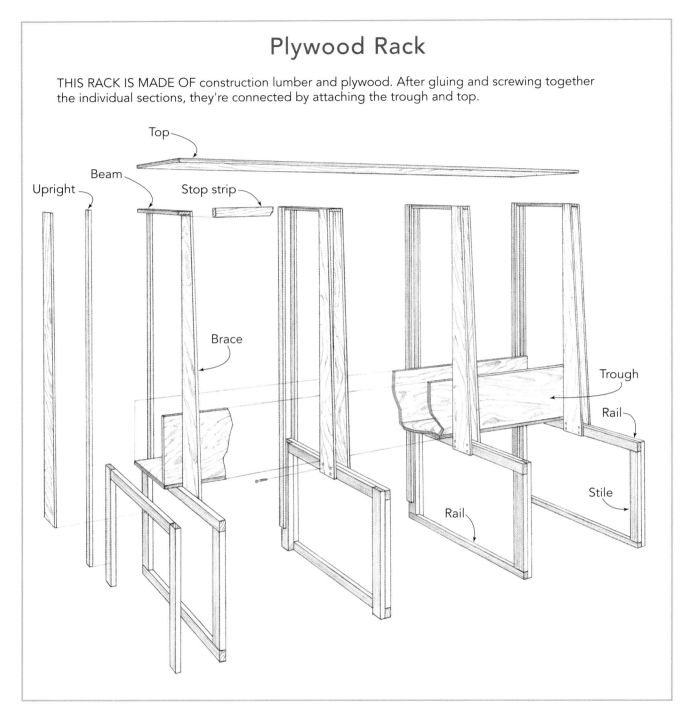

Assembling the Rack

1. Using a 12-in.-wide scrap of plywood as a stand-in spacer for the trough, glue and screw the braces to the upper frame rails and then screw them to the beams.

2. Saw the plywood pieces for the trough and the top. You can use thicker plywood for the trough walls, if you like, but it will slightly reduce your storage area.

3. Screw the trough bottom to the frames. You can temporarily tack braces across the frames to hold them up while you're doing this.

4. Finish up by attaching the top and screwing the trough walls to the braces and uprights. Make the stop strip and tack it in place to prevent items from slipping off the top.

CUT LIST FOR PLYWOOD RACK

8	Stiles	1¼" x 3¼" x 24"	Solid wood
8	Stiles	1¼" x 3¼" x 19½"	Solid wood
4	Rails	1¼" x 3¼" x 36"	Solid wood
4	Rails	1¼" x 3¼" x 29½"	Solid wood
4	Rails	1¼" x 1¼" x 36"	Solid wood
8	Uprights	¾" x 2" x 72½"	Solid wood
8	Braces	¾" x 5½" x 55¼"	Plywood
4	Beams	1¼" x 2½" x 16¼"	Solid wood
1	Top	¾" x 16¼" x 96"	Plywood
1	Trough bottom	¾" x 12" x 94½"	Plywood
2	Trough walls	¼" x 12" x 94½"	Plywood
1	Stop strip	¾" x 2½" x 96"	Plywood

PHOTO C: Saw the angled braces with a portable circular saw guided by a plywood straight edge.

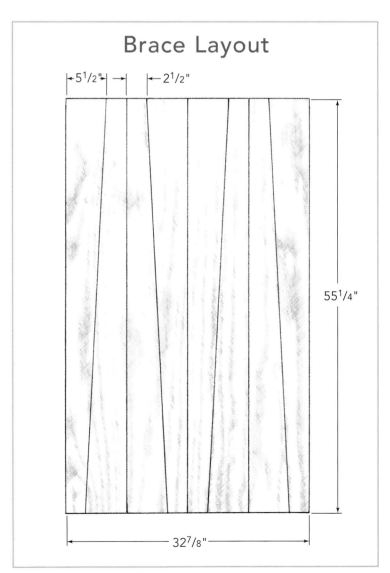

Brace Layout

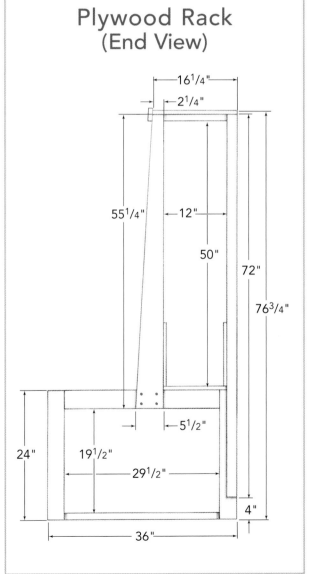

Plywood Rack (End View)

A properly equipped table-saw work-station provides quick access to all of the blades, tools, and accessories you'll need when using the saw. It can also do double or triple duty as an assembly station or router table.

Table-Saw Station

THE TABLE SAW IS ARGUABLY the most important machine in a typical woodshop. Because it is so central to the shop, it makes sense to outfit it as a primary workstation. As such, it should include the types of projects you'll find in this chapter: a good outfeed table, a crosscut sled, and storage for your table-saw tools and accessories.

These projects are important for efficiency, accuracy, and safety. Extension tables, for example, provide support for workpieces throughout the entirety of the cut, which results in more accurate cuts while preventing workpieces from falling after leaving the saw table or tipping off the table during the cut and possibly placing you in an awkward position over a spinning blade. Extension tables can also serve as assembly tables or staging platforms for workpieces in process.

A good crosscut sled is important because the small miter gauge supplied with the saw is woefully inadequate for feeding large workpieces through the blade. A crosscut sled allows you to accurately and safely feed long boards and wide panels across the saw tabletop. A sled can also be outfitted with stop blocks for quick repetitive sawing of multiples.

Storage for table-saw tools and accessories is critical for organization as well as protection of the tools. At the very least, you need safe storage for your blades and other cutters, which can represent a serious investment. You don't want them strewn about the shop, chipping their teeth on other metal tools or work surfaces. But for maximum efficiency, it's best that your table-saw workstation includes storage for all of those items attendant to a table saw, including blades, dado heads, saw wrenches, miter gauges, throat plates, featherboards, etc. Otherwise, you waste time traipsing all over the shop gathering these things as you need them.

Whatever sort of storage solutions you choose, it's helpful to gather together all the items you want to include, then design your storage units to accommodate them—as well as probable future acquisitions.

BLADE CABINET

SAWBLADES GENERALLY represent a considerable investment in tooling; a set of premium carbide blades can easily add up to hundreds of dollars. To protect your blades, they need to be kept sharp and rust free. Beware of hanging bunches of blades together on a nail, as the brittle carbide teeth can be easily damaged from hitting each other. It's much safer to keep blades separated in a box or cabinet.

This blade cabinet not only protects my blades, it provides easy access as well. Each blade rests on a pullout panel made of ¼-in.-thick Peg-Board, which slides in slots cut into plywood inserts that are tacked to the cabinet sides. The Peg-Board holes allow any ambient moisture in the cabinet to be absorbed by desiccant packages placed in the bottom compartment. The inset door keeps the cabinet relatively airtight. Thick, solid-wood edging dresses up the cabinet, while providing good screw purchase for the hinges.

Blade Cabinet

THE CASE SIDES ARE JOINED to the top and bottom with rabbet-and-dado joints. The back is inset into a rabbet that's cut after the case is assembled. the plywood edges on the case front and door are covered with solid-wood edging. The inserts are dadoed and then tacked to the cabinet sides.

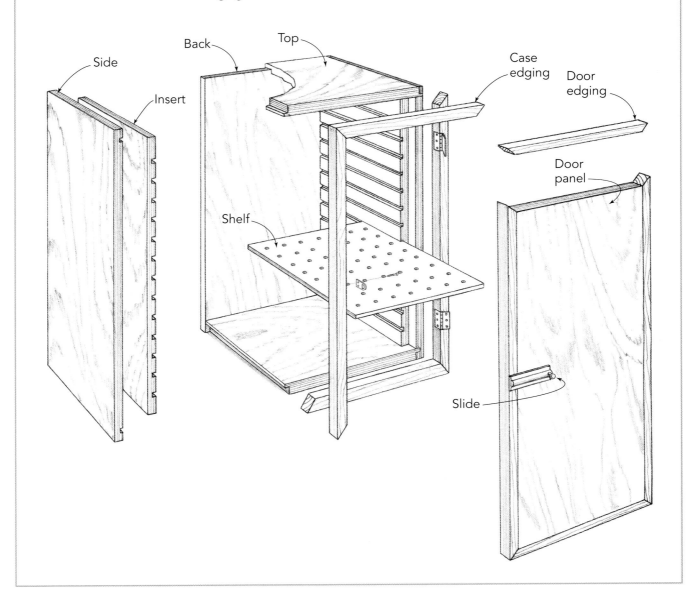

I made the cabinet from shop-grade ¾-in.-thick birch plywood, along with a bit of solid birch for edging. The door is hung on butt hinges and is latched with a brass slide bolt. The cabinet can easily be upsized to accommodate more blades or larger-diameter blades; if you currently have only a small collection, allow enough space for future acquisitions.

Making the Parts and Cutting the Joints

1. Lay out your plywood and saw the sides, top, bottom, inserts, and door panel to size. Cut the back a bit oversize for right now. Make sure to rip away the plywood factory edges to leave clean ones for attaching the solid-wood edging.

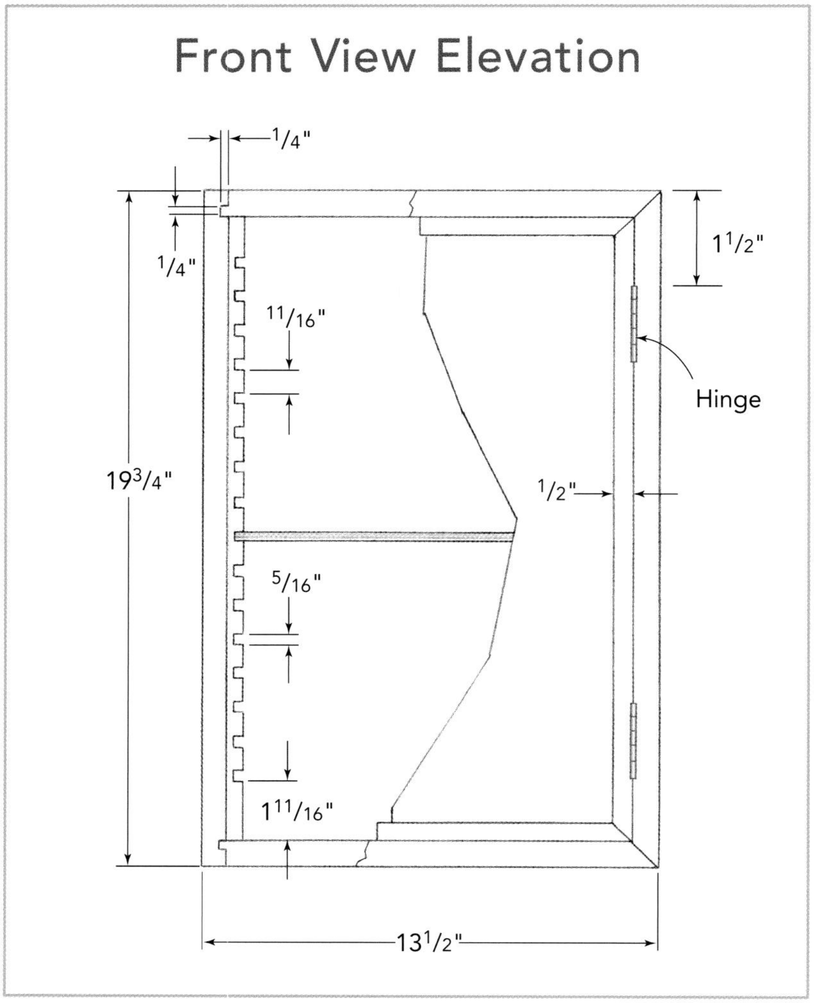

2. Saw or rout the ¼-in. by ¼-in. dadoes in the case sides.

3. Cut a rabbet on each end of the top and bottom to create the ¼-in. by ¼-in. tongue. Aim for a snug fit in the dadoes.

4. Dry-clamp the sides to the top and bottom to check the joint fits. With the unit clamped up, rout a ½-in.-deep by ⅜-in.-wide rabbet in the rear edges to accept the case back. Trim the back for a snug fit in the rabbets.

Cutting the Hinge Mortises and Assembling the Case

1. Lay out, rout, and chisel the hinge mortises in the case sides (see the drawing "Front View Elevation" at left). It's important to do this now, as the assembled case impedes router access.

2. Glue the sides to the top and bottom, making sure the rabbeted edge at the rear is flush. Insert the unglued back into its rabbets to hold the case square while the glue dries.

TIP

When fitting and gluing the edging to a case, align the inner edges closely, leaving most of the overhang on the exterior where it's easier to trim flush to the case.

CUT LIST FOR BLADE CABINET

2	Sides	¾" x 11½" x 19¾"	Hardwood plywood
2	Tops/bottoms	¾" x 11½" x 12½"	Hardwood plywood
2	Inserts	½" x 11" x 18¼"	Hardwood plywood
1	Back	½" x 12¾" x 19"	Hardwood plywood
1	Door panel	¾" x 11½" x 17⅜"	Hardwood plywood
17	Shelves	¼" x 10⅞" x 11⁷⁄₁₆"	Peg-Board
2	Case edgings	¾" x ¾" x 19¾"	Solid wood
2	Case edgings	¾" x ¾" x 13½"	Solid wood
2	Door edgings	½" x ¾" x 12"	Solid wood
2	Door edgings	½" x ¾" x 18¼"	Solid wood
Hardware			
2	Butt hinges	2" x 1⅜"	
1	Slide bolt	⅝" x 2"	

Making and Applying the Edging and Inserts

1. Mill the ½-in.-thick case edging, making it about ½ in. wider than the ¾-in.-thick plywood so you can trim it flush after attaching it (bottom photo on p. 127 and the photo on p. 128).

2. Fit the edging pieces. I mitered the corners although you could butt them together instead. Glue the edging to the case, clamping or nailing it in place.

3. Mill and fit the edging pieces to the door panel. Again, make the edging a bit fatter than the door panel. Glue the pieces on in opposing pairs in two steps, using the unglued set to align the pair that you glue on first.

4. Using a flush-trim router bit, trim the case and door edging flush to the plywood (see the top left photo on p. 109). Plane, scrape, or sand afterward to smooth the joints.

5. Lay out and cut the dadoes in the inserts. I sawed them using a dado head on the table saw, but you could rout them instead, guiding the router with a straight edge. Using 1-in. nails, tack the inserts to the case sides.

Installing the Door, Hardware, and Shelves

1. Trim the door so it's 1/16 in. smaller than its opening. Install the hinges into their mortises in the case side. Set the door on 1/16-in.-thick

TIP

Brass screw heads can snap off during installation, even in pilot holes. To prevent this, first prethread the screw holes using a steel screw.

PHOTO A: After trimming the inset door enough to slip it in its opening, press its edge against the hinge that's installed in the case mortise. Lay a sharp knife blade against the hinge leaf, and press the blade into the door edge to transfer the hinge-mortise location to the door.

shims in its opening, and press it against the hinges. Use a knife to transfer the location to the edge of the door (see photo A on p. 53).

2. Remove the hinges from the case, align them to your knife marks, and trace their outlines onto the door edge using a sharp knife. Rout and chisel the door mortises.

3. Install the door using only one screw per hinge leaf, and check the fit. Plane the door

edges if necessary to achieve a ⅟₁₆-in. gap all around. When you're happy with the fit, install the hinges using all their screws.

4. Finish up by cutting the Peg-Board shelves and fitting them into the dadoes. Install a slide-bolt catch and you're done. If you like, you can give the unit a quick sanding and an exterior coat of oil.

A ROUTER-TABLE EXTENSION

A table saw can do double duty as a router table by mounting a router under a side table or outfeed table. If mounted in a side table, you can use your table-saw rip fence as a router fence, as shown in the photo below. You can also mount a router in an outfeed table if, for example, your

table-saw side table abuts a wall, preventing access to the end of the side table (see the photo on p. 48) The only disadvantage to a router mounted in an outfeed table is that the fence and projecting bit can prevent ripping of long boards.

OUTFEED TABLE

HERE'S A SIMPLE BUT STRONG outfeed table that will do more than just support workpieces as they're sawn. Because this table has a flat, glue-resistant top and adjustable leveling feet, it serves as a great assembly table. Another feature of this freestanding unit is that it can be pulled away from the saw for initial crosscutting of large sheet goods. With the table sitting a foot or so from the table saw, a portable circular saw can travel safely across the gap with the sheet fully supported on the table and saw (see the photo on p. 33). No more cutting sheets on 2x4s lying on the floor or setting up four sawhorses to prevent large offcuts from pinching the kerf or crashing to the floor.

I made this table from oak, but any hardwood will do. Mortise-and-tenon apron joints provide plenty of strength without

CUT LIST FOR OUTFEED TABLE

4	Legs	2" x 2" x 32¾"	Solid wood
2	Side rails	1" x 3½" x 39⅜"	Solid wood
2	End rails	1" x 3½" x 43⅞"	Solid wood
1	Center rail	1" x 3½" x 38"	Solid wood
2	Side edgings	¼" x ¾" x 44"	Solid wood
2	End edgings	¼" x ¾" x 49¼"	Solid wood
1	Top panel	¾" x 44" x 48¾"	MCP or MDF
Hardware			
4	Lag screws	⅜" x 3"	

requiring lower stretchers, which would prevent rolling a compressor or other tool underneath for storage. Lag screws installed in the legs allow easy leveling for wavy shop floors (as though there is any other type). I made the top with a piece of Melamine®-coated particleboard (MCP), but you could cover a sheet of MDF with plastic laminate instead. Plywood works, too, but it may not stay as flat. I attached the top with pocket screws to hold it flat to the aprons and center rail.

I calculated the length of this top so that the far end would be 50 in. from the trailing

Outfeed Table

THE BASE, CONSISTING OF THE LEGS AND RAILS, is made of straight-grained, quartersawn stock to prevent warpage. The side and end rails join to the legs with mortise-and-tenon joints. The center rail is biscuited in place, although you could use screws. The top is made from high-quality particleboard—like MDF or MCP—for flatness, and it is simply screwed to the rails.

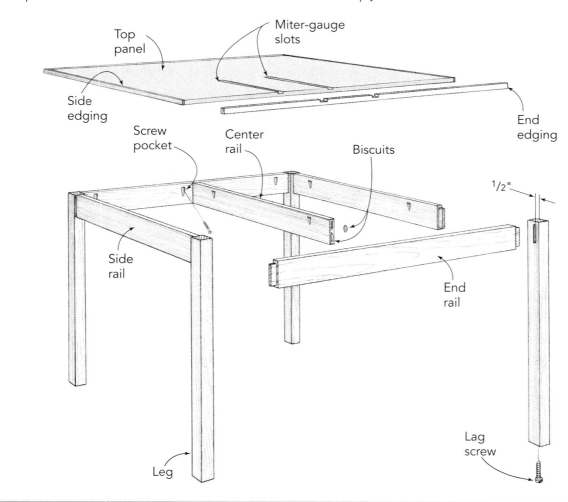

end of my table-saw blade, to prevent an 8-ft.-long sheet from tipping after a full-length ripcut. The table overhang provides a wide clamping ledge. To determine the proper length of the legs for your table, subtract 1¾ in. from the height of your table saw—¾ in. for the thickness of the top and 1 in. of space for leveling with the lag screws.

Building the Base

1. Plane, joint, rip, and crosscut the legs and rails to size. Leave the center rail a bit oversize in length for now. Also mill an extra couple of inches worth of leg stock for use as a drilling jig later. Because an extension/assembly table needs to be flat, it's important to mill the stock straight, flat, and square. To prevent warp, use straight-grained riftsawn or quartersawn stock.

2. Cut the ½-in. by 1½-in. by 2¾-in. mortises in the legs (see the drawing "Mortise and Tenon Detail" at right). It's easiest to rout them using a router edge guide, but you could drill and chop them out instead (see photo B on p. 58).

3. Saw the apron tenons to fit snugly in their mortises.

4. Dry-assemble the aprons and legs to make sure the joints are all snug and that the aprons line up to the tops of the legs. Trim the top edges of the tenons if necessary to get them to line up. Lay the center rail across the aprons, mark it to final length, and cut it.

5. Disassemble the parts, and lay out and cut the biscuit slots for joining the center rail to the aprons. If you don't have a biscuit joiner, you could screw through the end rail into the center rail instead during assembly.

6. Drill the screw pocket holes for attaching the top later. If you don't have a pocket-hole jig, you could attach wooden cleats to the aprons and rails through which you could drive screws to attach the top later.

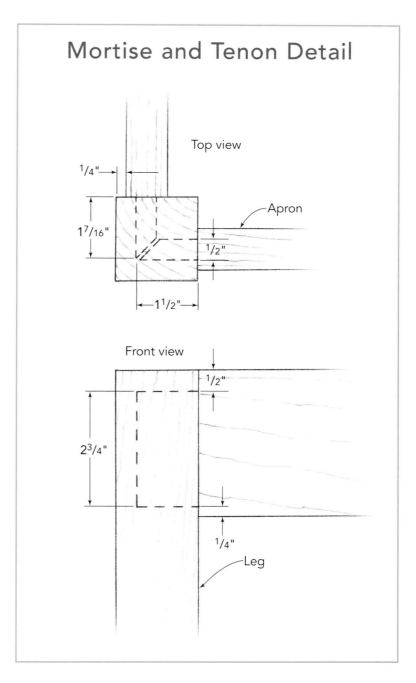

Mortise and Tenon Detail

Top view

Front view

7. Glue and clamp the legs to the end rails, making sure that the parts are square to each other under clamp pressure and that the tops of the rails and legs line up. Align the clamp screws with the centerline of the rail to prevent cocking the legs out of square. Let the glue dry thoroughly.

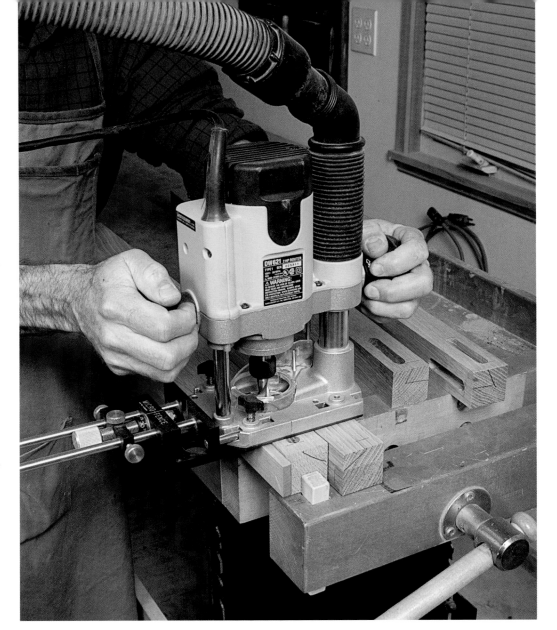

PHOTO B: Rout the leg mortises using a plunge router outfitted with an upcut spiral bit and an edge guide. Plunge to full depth at both ends of the mortise, and remove the rest of the material by making successive shallow passes.

TIP

To clean up excess glue during assembly, wipe it off immediately with a clean rag and clean water. When the water gets cloudy, replace it to prevent wiping diluted glue into the wood pores and causing finishing problems. Alternatively, you can wait until the drying glue gets rubbery and then trim it off with a sharp chisel.

8. Glue and clamp the end assemblies to the center rail and side rails, again making sure that the top edges align with the tops of the legs. If you are attaching the center rail with screws instead of biscuits, do that now. To hide the screws, counterbore the holes and fill them with wooden plugs trimmed flush to the surface.

9. Cut at least a 1-in.-long section from the excess leg stock that you milled. Using the drill press, bore a hole through the axis of the block to guide the drill bit that you'll use for installing the lag-screw levelers. Clamp the block to the bottom of each leg and drill the lag-screw holes.

10. Install the lag screws, and sand the base to remove sharp corners and edges.

Making the Top

1. Cut the top panel to size. Make sure to trim away any factory edges in the process to create a clean, square edge for attaching the solid-wood edging.

2. Mill the edging strips, making them just a hair oversize in length and just a bit wider than the thickness of the top panel.

3. Glue on the side edging. I clamped it in place using pipe clamps and thick cauls, but you could tack it on with brads instead. After the glue dries, trim the ends flush with the panel edges and attach the end edging. Finish the edging by trimming it flush to the panel faces using a router or scraper. Give it a light sanding.

4. Screw the top to the rails, keeping the overhang equal on all edges.

5. Place the table against your table saw, and level it so it's about 1/16 in. below your saw table. Mark out the miter-gauge slots. They should be long enough to allow full travel of your miter gauge and any crosscut sleds or other jigs that use the slots. I made my slots 1 in. wide and just a bit deeper than my saw's slots.

6. Rout the slots using a straight board to guide your router.

7. I finished up by applying one coat of wiping varnish. (It ain't no piano.)

TABLE-SAW KILL SWITCHES

For general safety and convenience when operating a table saw, consider outfitting it with a foot or knee kill switch. A stock table-saw switch is not often accessible, which can be dangerous if you need to shut the saw off at a moment's notice. Fortunately, it's not difficult to make and install a shopmade mechanism that allows you to shut off your saw quickly. The design of the mechanism will depend on the type of switch you have. Andy Rae hinged to the switch box a length of wood that presses against the off switch when pushed with his foot (see the photo at left). Walt Segl's knee switch is accessible from any position in front of the saw body (see the photo below).

CROSSCUT SLED

PHOTO C: A crosscut sled runs in the saw's miter-gauge slots and provides a long fence and base for carrying large workpieces safely and accurately through the blade.

THE STOCK MITER GAUGE that comes with a table saw is too small for crosscutting panels and long workpieces. To make the most of your table saw's crosscutting capabilities, you need a way to feed large, long stock safely and accurately through the blade. A crosscut sled fits the bill nicely. The sled rides in the saw's miter-gauge slots and provides solid support and backup for big workpieces (see photo C). It's not difficult to make a crosscut sled, but it needs to be constructed in a certain order, as follows. (Note: Make sure your sawblade is precisely aligned to its miter-gauge slots before proceeding. If you align it afterward, you'll have to readjust the sled fence for square cuts.)

Making the Pieces

1. Saw the panel from a piece of flat ½-in.-thick hardwood plywood. You can make the sled any size you like. (The one shown here is sized to handle typical 24-in.-deep cabinet case pieces.) Just make sure that your finished sled will overhang the left side of your saw tabletop by at least 1 in.

2. Mill and shape the fence and brace from a stable hardwood like mahogany. It's critical that the fence be absolutely straight and that its bottom edge is square to its inner face. To reduce weight, the ends of the brace and fence are stepped down. The left end of the fence is higher to accommodate a stop-block extension bar. Edges are rounded for comfort. A ⅛-in. by ⅛-in. rabbet in the fence provides clearance for sawdust buildup.

CROSSCUT SLED

THE PANEL IS MADE of $1/2$"-thick hardwood plywood. The fence and brace are straight-grained hardwood. The runners can be made of hardwood, plastic, or metal. The stop block butts against a similar block mounted on the edge of the saw table and prevents the sled from traveling past the blade at top dead center.

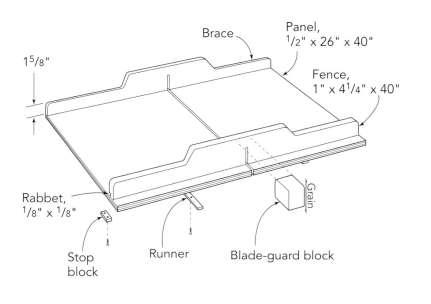

- Brace
- Panel, $1/2$" x 26" x 40"
- Fence, 1" x $4^{1}/4$" x 40"
- $1^{5}/8$"
- Rabbet, $1/8$" x $1/8$"
- Stop block
- Runner
- Blade-guard block
- Grain

PHOTO D: A scraper blade works great for trimming the sled runners for an easy, sliding fit in the saw's miter-gauge slots. Shave a bit at a time from any area that shows glossy rub spots from travel in the slots.

3. Mill hardwood runners to fit in the miter-gauge slots. They should fit the slots snugly from side to side, but they should be slightly shallower than the slots so the runners don't rub on the bottom.

4. Make and shape the blade-guard block, orienting the grain vertically for a long-grain-to-long-grain glue joint with the fence (see the drawing "Crosscut Sled" above).

Assembling and Fitting the Sled

1. Attach the brace to the panel with counter-sunk screws, avoiding the blade's path.

2. Place the runners in their slots, and lay the panel on top of them. Set the rip fence to ensure that when the panel is placed against it, the left edge overhangs the saw by about 1 in.

CUT LIST FOR CROSSCUT SLED

1	Panel	$1/2$" x 26" x 40"	Hardwood plywood
1	Brace	1" x $4^{1}/4$" x 40"	Solid wood
1	Fence	1" x $4^{1}/4$" x 40"	Solid wood
2	Runners	$5/16$" x $3/4$" x 26"	Solid wood
1	Blade guard	$1^{3}/4$" x 4" x $3^{3}/4$"	Solid wood

3. With the panel against the fence, drive brads through the panel into the runners. Leave the brad heads proud for easy removal later. Flip the sled upside down, and attach the runners from underneath with counter-sunk flathead screws.

4. Place the sled back into its slots, and trim the edges of the runners as necessary to create an easy, sliding fit with no side-to-side play. A rabbet plane or scraper is the best

PHOTO E: With the fence attached with one screw at the far right end, square it to the blade and then clamp the left end of the fence to the panel. Make test cuts, adjusting the angle of the fence as necessary, before screwing it to the panel.

tool for the job (see photo D on p. 61) but you can also use a sanding block or scrape the runners with the tip of a sharp chisel. Go easy, working a bit at a time, while checking the runners for rub marks.

5. Attach the fence (with one screw only) at the far right end. Inset the fence about ¾ in. from the front edge of the panel. Clamp the left end to the panel.

Adjusting the Rear Fence

1. Raise the sawblade about 2 in. above the table, and cut most of the way across the panel, stopping a couple of inches shy of its front edge.

2. Using an accurate square, adjust the fence until it's perpendicular to the kerf you just cut in the panel. Then tightly clamp the left end of the fence to the panel (see photo E).

3. Make a test crosscut using a scrap of wood that has absolutely parallel edges. After making the cut, flip one of the halves upside down, and butt the sawn ends together with the long edges against the fence. If the ends don't meet perfectly, readjust the angle of the fence a bit and try again. When you get a square cut, screw the fence to the panel.

Finishing Up

1. For safety, the sled should stop when the top of the blade reaches the inside face of the fence. To stop the sled, you can screw a stop block to its underside and bolt a mating stop block to the edge of the saw table at the proper location. If using an outfeed table, simply make its miter-gauge slots short enough to stop the sled's travel at the proper distance.

2. Glue the blade-guard block to the fence, and finish up by waxing the runners for easy travel in their slots.

A MOBILE TABLE-SAW CABINET

The space under the side extension table is the ideal spot for a storage cabinet for blades, throat plates, squares, and other indispensable table-saw accoutrements. If the access door on your saw opens into that space, you can outfit the cabinet with wheels for easy removal when you need to get into the saw body. Walt Segl's cabinet shown here includes brackets on the top, for holding his after-market miter gauge, and slotted blocks on the front, to hold his blade wrenches.

TABLE-SAW
ACCESSORIES CABINET

ONE OF THE BEST WAYS to make use of the area under your side extension table is to build a cabinet that suits the space. A cabinet can provide stout support for the table, as well as offer housing to help manage your tools and supplies. You can customize a cabinet with all sorts of compartments for specific tools and accessories, but a simple drawer cabinet provides plenty of flexibility. Andy Rae built this cabinet with a bank of drawers in front and a bank in the rear for easy access and lots of storage.

Rae used hardwood plywood for the case and for the base on which it sits. A central divider biscuited to the sides keeps the cabinet strong and square. He used maple for the edging and drawers. The drawer fronts are joined to the sides with sliding dovetails, a strong joint that can withstand a lot of tugging and abuse. The drawers are mounted using commercial, full-extension slides, and the 4-in.-tall base allows plenty of broom clearance for sweeping up sawdust beneath. You may need to adjust the height of the base to suit the height of your extension table.

Making the Case

Make the case first so you can fit the drawers to it. If you don't have a biscuit joiner for attaching the divider, you can dado the case sides instead, adjusting the width of the divider accordingly.

1. Lay out and saw the sides, top, and bottom to size. At the same time, make the pieces for the base, remembering to adjust its height if necessary to suit your extension table.

2. Saw or rout the ⅜-in. by ¾-in. rabbets in the top and bottom edges of the sides to accept the top and bottom panels. Because

Table-Saw Accessories Cabinet

THE CASE IS MADE OF HARDWOOD PLYWOOD, with a center divider biscuited between the sides to hold the cabinet square. The base is made separately and then screwed on. The plywood edges are covered with solid wood. The drawers—made with sliding dovetails and dado joints—are mounted on commercial slides.

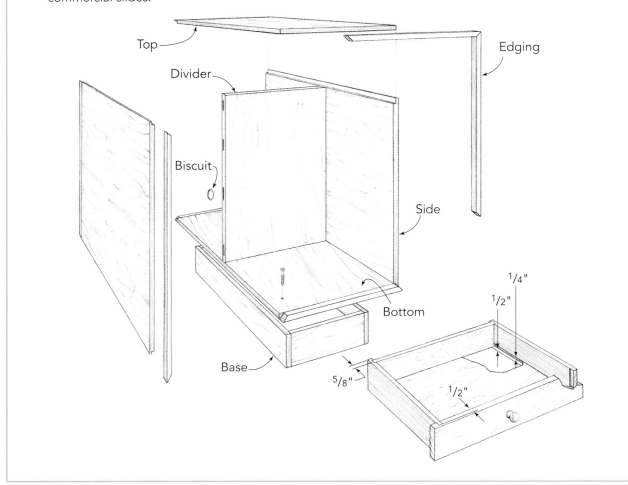

hardwood plywood is seldom its stated thickness, it's important to make sure that the thickness of the tongue is ⅜ in. rather than measuring the depth of the rabbet, which can lead to inaccurate cabinet width.

3. Dry-clamp the sides to the top and bottom. Take exact measurements for the divider, and cut it to size.

4. Lay out and cut the biscuit slots in the divider as well as their mating slots in the case sides (see photo F on p. 66). Dry-assemble the case to check the fit of the joints.

5. Glue and clamp the case together, keeping the clamp screws centered over the edges of the top and bottom to prevent bowing in the sides. Alternatively, you could either glue and nail or screw the parts together, filling the holes later if you choose. Assemble the base now, too.

6. Mill strips for the edging, leaving it a bit fatter in width than the thickness of the plywood. Fit the pieces to the front and back, mitering them at the corners. Glue and clamp or nail the edging in place. After the glue dries, rout the edging flush using a flush-trim router bit.

7. Screw the base to the case.

CUT LIST FOR TABLE-SAW ACCESSORIES CABINET

Case

2	Tops/Bottoms	¾" x 19¼" x 34¼"	Hardwood plywood
2	Sides	¾" x 34¼" x 27"	Hardwood plywood
1	Divider	¾" x 18½" x 25½"	Hardwood plywood
2	Bases	¾" x 4" x 12½"	Hardwood plywood
2	Bases	¾" x 4" x 29¾"	Hardwood plywood

Drawers

4	Fronts	¾" x 5¼" x 18½"	Solid wood
4	Fronts	¾" x 7½" x 18½"	Solid wood
8	Sides	½" x 5¼" x 16½"	Solid wood
8	Sides	½" x 7½" x 16½"	Solid wood
4	Backs	½" x 4½" x 17"	Solid wood
4	Backs	½" x 6¾" x 17"	Solid wood
8	Bottoms	½" x 15⅝" x 17"	Hardwood plywood

Elevations

Front/back view

Side view (with side removed)

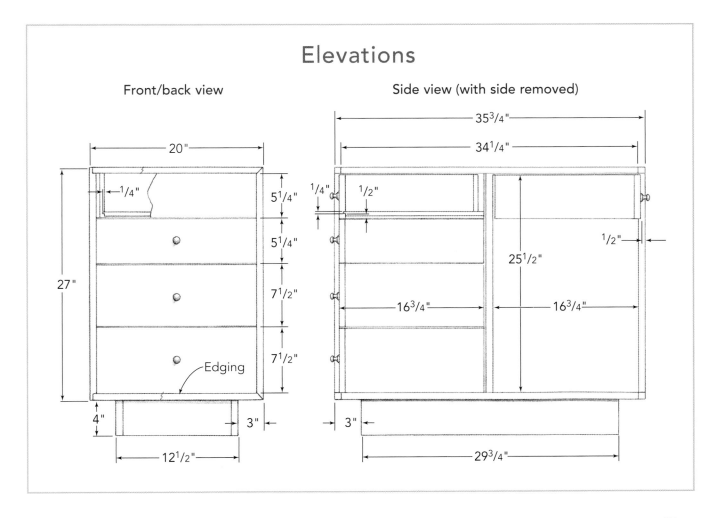

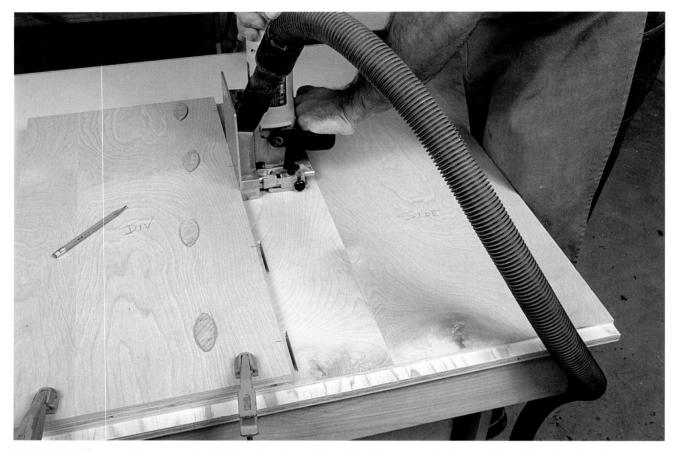

PHOTO F: After marking out the divider location, clamp it adjacent to its layout line. Cut the slots in the case side registering the biscuit-joiner base against the divider. Afterward, cut the slots in the end of the divider.

TIP

Don't overlook good overhead lighting for your saw. Fluorescent fixtures broadcast good ambient light, but to really see what you're doing, it's best to augment that with incandescent lighting aimed at the area around the blade.

Making the Drawers

The drawer box must be exactly 1 in. less than the width of the case opening to accommodate the drawer slides.

1. Joint, plane, and rip the stock for the drawer parts. Make some extra stock for setting up cuts later. Saw the pieces to length, crosscutting the fronts close to their final length. If the drawer fronts are too long, the dovetail slots will be too far apart, splaying the drawer sides outward near the drawer opening and binding the operation of the drawer slides.

2. Carefully lay out the dovetail slots on one of the drawer fronts, working from the center outward.

3. Set up your router table with a ¼-in.-dia. straight bit for wasting most of the dovetail slot. Set the bit to cut a hair less than ½ in. deep. Use your marked-out drawer front to set the fence the proper distance from the bit. Make a test cut in a piece of scrap, and compare it to the layout lines on your drawer front. Adjust the fence as necessary, and rout these starter slots in all of your drawer fronts.

4. Install a ½-in. dovetail bit in your table router, and adjust it for a ½-in.-deep cut. Rout your dovetail slots, carefully holding the workpiece against the fence while backing it up with a square piece of stock to support it and minimize exit tearout (see photo G on facing page).

5. Without changing the height of the bit, adjust the fence for shaping the tails on the drawer sides. Make test cuts in scrap, standing the scrap upright and first routing one side and then the other (see photo H). Test the fit in your slots. If the tail is too tight, tap the fence away from the bit, but remember that you only want to move it half the amount of the error, as you'll be routing both sides again. Once you've got the fit right, rout the tails on all of the drawer sides.

6. Rout or saw the ¼-in. by ½-in. dadoes in the drawer sides to accept the drawer backs. While you're at it, cut the ¼-in. drawer-bottom grooves in the front and sides, and rabbet the drawer bottoms to fit the grooves. A dado head on the table saw makes quick work of all this.

7. Dry-assemble the drawers and fit the bottoms. Glue up the drawers, inserting each bottom dry to hold the drawer square while the glue cures.

8. After the glue cures, set each drawer in turn on a flat surface and check for rock. If necessary, handplane opposing corners of the bottom until the drawer sits flat. Then plane the top edges parallel to the bottom edges.

9. Install the drawer bottoms, gluing them into the grooves of the drawer box for extra strength.

Installing the Drawers

To achieve the best fit, install the drawers one by one, fitting each and trimming its front to fit before moving on to the next drawer.

1. Beginning with a bottom drawer, install the case-half of each slide, making sure it's square to the case front. Set the front end of the slide 1¼ in. back from the case edges to recess the drawers ½ in., as shown in the drawing "Elevations" on p. 65.

2. Install the mating half of each slide onto the drawer, and mount the drawer in the case. If necessary, mark the edges of the drawer front to create a small, even gap adjacent to the case. Plane the drawer to your marks, and reinstall it to check the gaps.

3. Using the installed bottom drawer as a reference, install the next drawer up in the same fashion. Repeat the process for all

PHOTO G: After routing a groove with a straight bit to remove most of the waste, finish up the dovetail slot by routing it with a ½-in. dovetail bit. Hold the workpiece firmly against the fence while backing it up with a square piece of stock to support it and minimize exit tearout.

PHOTO H: Rout the mating tails by burying the bit the proper distance in the fence and feeding the drawer sides on end. Rout both faces, test the fit, and readjust the fence as necessary.

remaining drawers. If the drawers don't move smoothly, check the gap between the drawer and case sides. To reduce the gap, shim out the case slides; to increase it, sand or scrape the drawer sides.

4. Install the pulls, give the unit a light sanding, and apply a coat of finish if you like.

A well-thought-out drilling station includes a drill press with a versatile table, such as Craig Bentzley's shopmade table shown here with its adjustable fence, sliding stops, and hold-downs. Bit storage nearby is crucial to efficiency, as is a staging table or bench for holding workpieces.

DRILLING STATIONS

EXT TO SAWING, drilling is one of the most common operations performed in the woodshop. It is crucial when preparing parts for assembly with screws and other hardware. Workpieces often must be drilled for screw pilot and clearance holes as well as countersinks and counterbores. Parts joined with dowels or round tenons must be accurately bored as well, usually at a specific angle. Parts can also be partially shaped by drilling—for example, when cutting the radiused sections of ogee bracket feet or other scrollwork with arcs.

A drilling workstation can expedite all of these processes. The heart of the workstation is the drill press, but a station also serves as a dedicated space to store and organize your various portable drills and accessories. In this chapter, we'll look at auxiliary drill-press tables that will greatly expand the capabilities of your drill press. You'll also find some great ideas for storing your drills, bits, and accessories.

A drill press is a virtual necessity in a woodshop, but the typical drill-press table is inadequate in a number of ways. For one, the table is too small and doesn't provide an easy way to register workpieces. For another, the metal table can ruin a bit if your depth stop slips or if you forget to set it.

To make the most of a drill press, you'll want a well-designed auxiliary table like one of those in this chapter. You'll find that a good auxiliary table and fence can be outfitted to perform all kinds of accurate, repetitive operations. For example, a fence saves time and ensures accuracy when drilling a row of holes parallel to the edge of a workpiece. Incorporating flip stops on the fence makes repeatability even more versatile, and T-tracks installed in the table will accept hold-down and other small fixtures. The tilting-table project in this chapter makes drilling angled holes a snap, and the slip-on table may be just the thing you need for quick conversions back to the stock metal table.

DRILL RACK

T O KEEP MY PORTABLE DRILLS at the ready, I designed and made this wall-mounted rack that accommodates my seven drills, with space for an addition down the line. The unit includes an upper shelf to hold a right-angle drill and a battery charger. The drill board angles outward to present the handles for an easy grab. Each drill chuck fits easily, but not too loosely, in its custom-size hole. The unit is screwed together without glue so you can disassemble it later, if necessary, to add or enlarge holes for new drills.

This rack is easy to make but may involve a bit of customization to accommodate your particular drills, especially if they're large. The dimensions of this rack should work for most drills, but check to make sure that it suits all of yours. I've included suggestions here on how to lay out the rack for your drills.

Making the Rack

1. As with any wall-hung unit, mark the wall-stud spacing in the area you want to hang the unit. Make sure the rack will overlay at least two studs.

2. Check the width of battery chargers or any other tools or accessories that you want the shelf to hold. If your charger is much wider than 4 in., you'll need to increase the depth of both the shelf and the drill board. If your charger is very wide, you could build a short shelf at one end or else omit the shelf entirely. To play with the size of the design, draw a full-scale profile as a reference, and lay each of your drills over the drawing (see the drawing "Drill Rack" End View at right).

3. Cut the pieces to size. When ripping the drill board, begin by making it about ¼ in.

CUT LIST FOR DRILL RACK

1	Backboard	¾" x 7¼" x 30"
1	Drill board	1¼" x 5¼" x 30"
1	Shelf	¾" x 3¼" x 30"
1	Stop strip	¼" x 1¾" x 30"

oversize in width. Saw the bevel on the rear edge of the drill board. Save the offcut.

4. Mark the chuck-hole centerline on the drill board 1¾ in. from the outside edge, and dry-clamp the drill board and shelf to the backboard. Use the bevel-ripped offcut to create parallel faces for clamping the angled drill board (see photo A on p. 72). Space the chuck-hole centerlines by standing your drills in pairs next to each other with the cords wrapped around the bodies. Allow enough room to comfortably get your hand around each drill.

5. Determine the size of the holes you'll need for the drill board. I used a caliper to measure the widest section of each drill chuck, and bored a bunch of test holes in thick scrap to check the fit of each chuck in its hole. The chuck should slide in easily but not too loosely. On the drill board, I marked the appropriate diameter next to the hole location allotted to a specific drill.

6. Disassemble the unit, and drill the chuck holes on the drill press. I used multispur bits for drilling, but hole saws or spade bits would work, too.

7. Screw the shelf and drill board to the backboard using #8 by 2½-in. drywall screws. When drilling the pilot hole for the drill-board screws, favor the bottom edge of the backboard to prevent breaking out the top edge of the drill board (see the End View in the drawing "Drill Rack" at right). Ease sharp edges and corners with 100-grit sandpaper.

8. The rack is now ready to hang. I wiped a coat of oil on it first because, well, why not?

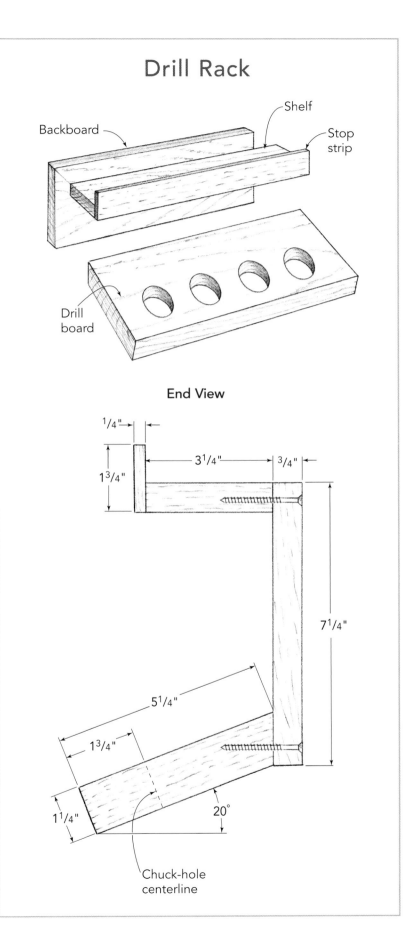

Drill Rack

Backboard · Shelf · Stop strip · Drill board

End View

1/4" · 1³/4" · 3¹/4" · 3/4" · 7¹/4" · 5¹/4" · 1³/4" · 1¹/4" · 20°

Chuck-hole centerline

PHOTO A: To determine how far apart to space your drill chuck holes, dry-clamp the unit together, and stand your cord-wrapped drills next to each other, allowing enough grab space between drills. Use a block drilled with test holes to determine the size of the hole needed for each individual drill.

STORING PORTABLE DRILLS

Portable hand drills can present a storage challenge. Although most cordless drills will stand upright, corded drills can be a problem. If you store them on a shelf or in a drawer, they tend to pile on each other and the cords inevitably end up in an ugly wrestling match. It's best if each drill has its own space while remaining immediately accessible for a quick draw.

One approach is to store drills in individual compartments, as Tony O'Malley does. He constructed wall-hung boxes with removable dividers that can be adjusted to accommodate various drills, nail guns, and other tools

(see the bottom photo at left). For a touch of the Wild West, you can make leather holsters for your drills, as Bob Whitley did (see the bottom photo at right).

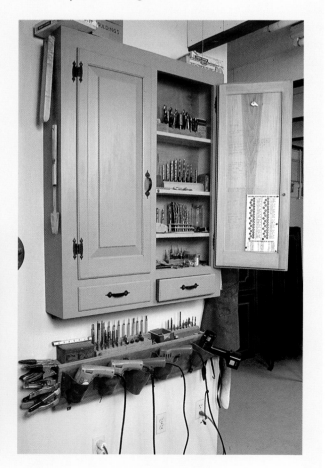

TILTING DRILL-PRESS TABLE

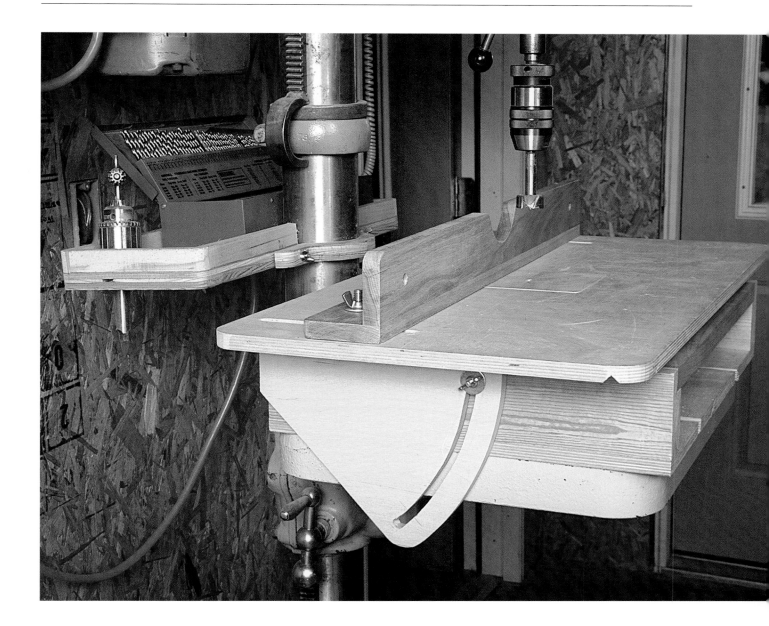

MIKE CALLIHAN GOT tired of having to make jigs to hold workpieces for angled boring because his stock drill-press table isn't adjustable for angles. To solve the problem, he designed this auxiliary drill-press table that tilts to any angle up to 45 degrees. The table is hinged to a base and employs slotted brackets, bolts, and wing nuts for setting the angle. A sacrificial insert plate minimizes exit tearout on a workpiece.

Callihan uses an inclinometer (a carpenter's tool available at building-supply stores) to set the angle (see photo B on p. 75). You could also use a bevel gauge to set the angle. After determining an angle, a specifically sized support block can be made for quick setup in the future. The dowel on the underside of the table provides single-point contact for accurate repeatability.

Tilting Drill-Press Table

THE TABLE IS CONSTRUCTED of three separate assemblies connected together. The top assembly consists of the top, sub-top, and brackets. The base is comprised of the sides, rails, and bottom panel. The fence is simply two boards connected at right angles. The top assembly is hinged to the base assembly, and the fence is connected to the top with carriage bolts in slots that allow for adjustment.

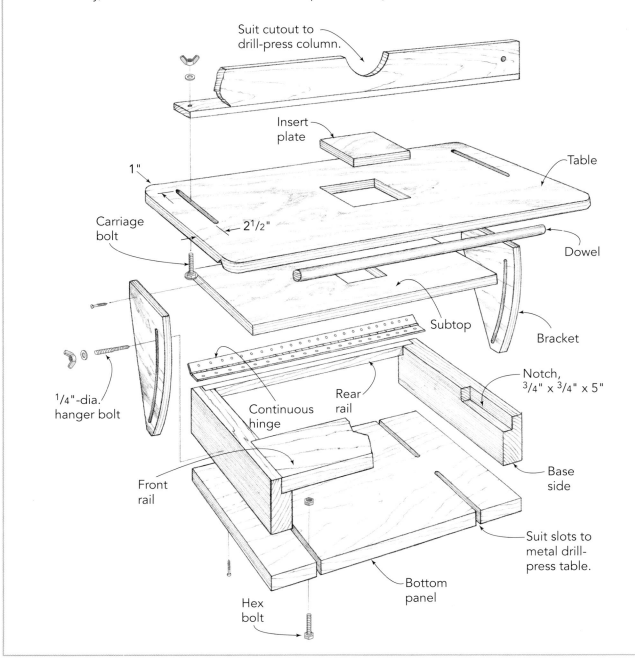

Suit cutout to drill-press column.

Insert plate

Table

1"

2¹/₂"

Carriage bolt

Dowel

¹/₄"-dia. hanger bolt

Subtop

Bracket

Notch, ³/₄" x ³/₄" x 5"

Continuous hinge

Rear rail

Base side

Front rail

Suit slots to metal drill-press table.

Hex bolt

Bottom panel

The arc-shaped cutout on the fence approximately matches the diameter of the drill-press column. Placing the fence so that the cutout nestles around the column allows maximum distance between the fence and chuck. Orienting the fence with the cutout upward, as in the drawing "Tilting Drill-Press Table" above provides chuck clearance for drilling near the edge of a workpiece using short bits.

For the plywood parts of his table, Callihan used ⅝-in.-thick Baltic birch plywood, but you could use ¾-in.-thick material instead. Obviously, you can make the table larger or smaller to suit your own needs. Just make sure that the brackets will be able to swing down past the metal drill-press table. You'll need to suit certain dimensions and spacings—such as the location of the insert plate and the bottom panel slots—to fit your own drill press.

Making the Table

1. Cut the table, subtop, and bottom panel to size. Use a square to draw a centerline front to back on all of the pieces.

2. Center the bottom panel side to side under the table with their front edges aligned, then center both pieces side to side on the metal table with the table pressed against the drill-press column. On the table, mark the location of your drill-press chuck. On the bottom panel, mark the locations of the bolts necessary to attach the bottom panel to your metal drill-press table.

3. Lay out and cut the opening in the table for the sacrificial insert. Callihan roughed out the opening with a jigsaw, and trimmed the edges straight with a router. For accuracy, he first made an insert plate, located it on the table, and then used hot-melt glue to attach blocks to the table against the edges of the insert. The blocks served as guides for a straight router bit with a top-mounted bearing (see photo C on p. 76).

4. Cut the base sides and rails to size, and notch the base sides to accept the rails. The notches are ¾ in. deep, extending halfway into the sides. Either glue and nail or screw the rails to the sides.

5. Align the rear edge of the subtop with the rear ends of the sides, then center the table

PHOTO B: Set the table angle using an inclinometer (shown here) or a bevel gauge. For quick future setups at that angle, make a support block that rests on the rail.

CUT LIST FOR TILTING DRILL-PRESS TABLE

Qty	Part	Dimensions	Material
1	Fence board	⅝" x 2½" x 29½"	Solid wood or hardwood plywood
1	Fence board	⅝" x 3" x 29½"	Solid wood or hardwood plywood
1	Table	⅝" x 16" x 30"	Hardwood plywood
1	Subtop	⅝" x 14" x 21"	Hardwood plywood
1	Insert plate	⅝" x 5" x 5"	Hardwood plywood
1	Dowel	¾" dia. x 20"	Wood
2	Brackets	⅝" x 8¼" x 10"	Hardwood plywood
2	Base sides	1½" x 3¼" x 16"	Solid wood
1	Rear rail	¾" x 1¼" x 19½"	Solid wood
1	Front rail	¾" x 5" x 19½"	Solid wood
1	Bottom panel	⅝" x 16" x 21"	Hardwood plywood

Hardware

Qty	Part	Spec
2	Carriage bolts	⅜-16 x 2 (with washer and wing nut)
1	Continuous hinge	1½" x 30"
2	Hanger bolts	5⁄16" x 2" (with washer and wing nut)
4	Hex bolt and nuts	Size for connection to metal drill-press table

PHOTO C: After sawing the opening for the insert slightly undersize, place the insert over the hole and surround it tightly with blocks affixed to the table using hot-melt glue. Then use a pattern-cutting bit guided by the blocks to finish the cut.

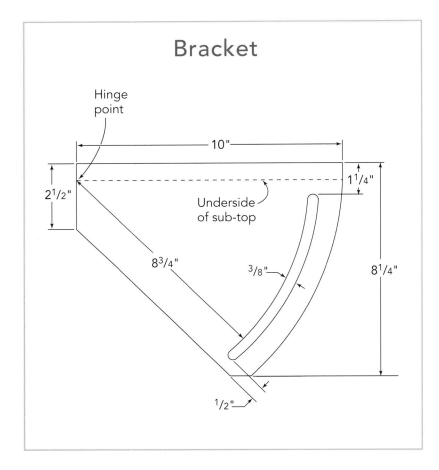

Bracket

Hinge point

10"

2¹/₂"

1¹/₄"

Underside of sub-top

8³/₄"

3/8"

8¹/₄"

1/2"

to allow the square section under the bolt head to slide easily but narrow enough to prevent its spinning. The slots should begin about 1 in. from the rear edge and extend about 1 in. shy of the center of the insert cutout.

7. Using the table saw, cut a ⁵/₁₆-in.-deep V-groove on the underside of the table, 1 in. back from the front edge, to accept the dowel. Make sure that when the dowel is sitting in the groove it will not project beyond the underside of the subtop. Screw the dowel into the groove.

8. Lay out the brackets on a piece of plywood (see the drawing "Bracket" at left). Before cutting them to shape, rout the ⅜-in.-wide curved slots using a trammel to guide your router (see photo D on facing page). For the table to operate correctly, the trammel point will need to line up with the hinge barrel when assembling the table. Therefore, make sure that the pivot point extends down from the top edge of the bracket at a distance equal to the thickness of your subtop material.

9. Cut the brackets to shape, and screw them to the edge of the subtop, making sure that the rear edges all align.

10. Screw the subtop to the table from underneath, and hinge the subtop to the rear rail.

11. Cut slots in the bottom panel to attach it to your metal drill-press table. Screw the bottom panel to the base sides.

side to side on the subtop, aligning the front edge of the table with the front edge of the front rail. Trace around the insert opening onto the subtop, and lay out lines about ½ in. in from those lines. Use a jigsaw to cut to the inner lines to create the opening in the subtop.

6. Rout the slots in the table for the fence carriage bolts. Make the slots wide enough

12. Install the hanger bolts in the base sides at the top end of the bracket slots. Make your pilot holes large enough to allow easy insertion of these headless bolts.

13. Make the fence. It's a good idea to use quartersawn wood to minimize warping. When drilling the bolt holes in both pieces, use the drill press to ensure that the holes are perpendicular to the fence faces for easy adjustment. Make the diameter of the cutout slightly larger than the diameter of your drill-press column.

14. Attach the fence with carriage bolts, washers, and wing nuts, and mount the completed table to your drill press. When mounting the table, it's important to position the rear edge of the top far enough from the drill-press column to prevent binding when pivoting.

TIP

Temporarily threading a cap nut onto a hanger bolt will provide purchase for a wrench to screw the bolt in.

PHOTO D: After laying out the brackets, use a trammel to cut the curved slot before sawing the brackets to final shape.

STORAGE FOR BITS AND ACCESSORIES

Tool manufacturers make a lot of items that slip into a drill chuck. If you've been woodworking for any length of time, you've probably accumulated a collection of twist drill bits, Forstner bits, multispur bits, spade bits, hole saws, countersinks, drum sanders, etc. All of these small items need some kind of organized storage. For a collection of large bits, a simple, shallow cabinet will do the trick (see the top photo at right). For more versatile storage, a wall cabinet with compartments and drawers will make your tool searches easier (see the bottom photo at right). A cabinet that's outfitted with casters provides a machine stand, tool storage, and mobility all in one (see the bottom photo at left).

SLIP-ON AUXILIARY DRILL-PRESS TABLE

SOMETIMES IT'S GOOD to have an auxiliary drill-press table that removes easily so you can outfit your metal drill-press table for operations that require other setups, such as attaching a drill-press vise. Brian Boggs designed his table for just such easy removal. The table fits snugly onto his metal drill-press table without need for any fasteners to hold it in place. The 24-in. by 27½-in. auxiliary table provides plenty of support for large workpieces. It should even fit over a round table, as the cutout for the column at the rear of the table will keep it from rotating.

Boggs made his table entirely from ¾-in.-thick birch plywood. Obviously, the table design will have to be modified to suit your particular drill press. However, the drawing "Slip-On Auxiliary Drill-Press Table" on p. 80 shows the basic construction. Just suit the dimensions to your drill press. The following is the basic construction sequence along with a few tips for fitting.

Making the Table

1. Cut the top to whatever size suits you, and notch out its rear edge at the center to slip snugly around your drill-press column.

2. Determine the width of the sides by holding a plywood panel up against the underside of your metal drill-press table and measuring up to the underside of your auxiliary top. Add about ¹⁄₃₂ in. to that dimension, and cut the sides to width and length. The sides will be ¾ in. less in length than the top to account for the thickness of the front board.

3. Make the bottom panel. To determine its width, measure the width of your metal drill-press table and add 1¹⁄₁₆ in. This accounts for the two ¾-in.-thick sides plus ¹⁄₁₆ in. for

Slip-On Auxiliary Drill-Press Table

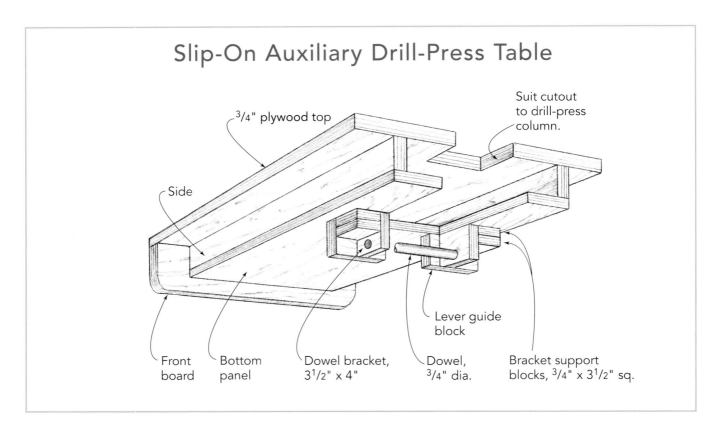

3/4" plywood top

Suit cutout to drill-press column.

Side

Lever guide block

Front board

Bottom panel

Dowel bracket, 3 1/2" x 4"

Dowel, 3/4" dia.

Bracket support blocks, 3/4" x 3 1/2" sq.

Table-Lift Mechanism

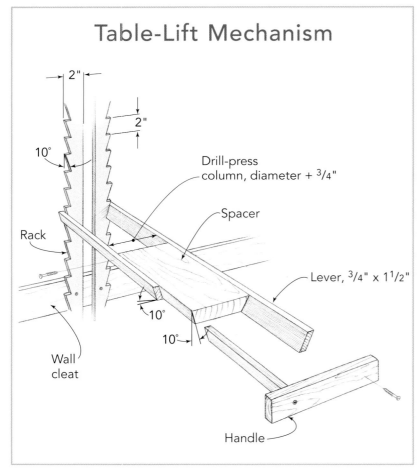

2"

2"

10°

Drill-press column, diameter + 3/4"

Spacer

Rack

Lever, 3/4" x 1 1/2"

10°

10°

Wall cleat

Handle

side-to-side clearance. Make any necessary cutouts in the panel to accommodate projecting parts on the underside of the metal table.

4. If you want to make an insert plate for the table, put the top in position, centering it on the metal table, and mark the location of the drill chuck. Using a jigsaw, make the cutout for the insert plate. Then make an insert plate that fits snugly in the cutout.

5. Cut the front board to size, and assemble the table using a few strategically placed screws. Slide the table in place to test the fit, make any adjustments, and install the rest of the screws.

Making the Table-Lift Mechanism

Boggs also devised a clever mechanism for easily raising and lowering his drill-press table. His drill press doesn't include a rack and crank for adjusting the table height, so he attached a lever assembly to the underside of his auxiliary table to allow easier height adjustment. The far end of the free-floating

lever assembly rests in notches on racks that are mounted to the wall behind the drill press (see photo E). Pulling upward on the lever causes it to contact the drill-press table mount. The lever then carries the weight of the table while raising or lowering it. (The metal table should be locked to the column once it has been adjusted.) When not in use, the lever can be removed or left to rest on the dowel mounted to the underside of the table.

The mechanism consists of three basic components: the wall-mounted racks, the lever assembly, and the dowel/bracket assembly attached to the underside of the table. They will probably have to be tailored to your specific drill press. Just follow the basic construction shown in the drawing "Slip-On Auxiliary Drill-Press Table" on the facing page.

Making the racks and lever assembly

1. Make the twin racks that mount to the wall. Boggs made his racks about 22 in. tall. Each rack is made from a 2-in.-wide piece of ¾-in.-thick hardwood plywood, notched with a bandsaw or jigsaw to create a series of 10-degree steps (see the drawing "Table-Lift Mechanism" on the facing page).

2. Measure the diameter of your drill-press column, and add ¾ in. to that to determine the width of the spacer. Make the spacer. Its length isn't critical; about 10 in. should be fine. Bevel both edges at 10 degrees.

3. Make the two levers from ¾-in. by 1½-in. stock, beveling the bottom edge of each at 10 degrees so they'll make full contact with the bottoms of the notches on the racks. The levers should extend from the wall to about 1 in. shy of the front of your drill-press table.

4. Screw the levers to the spacer. Locate the spacer to best suit the metal table mount on your particular drill press. Boggs places his spacer so that the round plate on the underside of his drill-press table is cradled between the two levers when they're lifted (see the photo on p. 75). If necessary, modify your lever assembly to make good contact with your table mount. Last, attach the lever assembly handle.

Making the lever-guide assembly and mounting the racks

The lever-guide assembly attached to the underside of the table consists of brackets, a dowel, and two guide blocks. The dowel provides a rest for the lever assembly, and the lever guide blocks keep the lever assembly centered.

PHOTO E: This shop-made lever-and-rack mechanism works great for drill presses with no table-height crank. When the lever assembly is inserted into the rack on the wall and lifted, it supports the weight of the table as it's raised or lowered on the drill-press column.

1. Make the lever-guide assembly based on the drawing "Slip-On Auxiliary Drill-Press Table" on p. 80. On Boggs's table, the dowel brackets are mounted to either side of the large cutout, with the lever guide blocks extending inward. If the bottom panel of your table doesn't have a wide cutout, you can omit the guide blocks, letting the dowel brackets serve as guides.

2. Mount a couple of horizontal cleats on the wall, screwing them to the wall studs that flank the area behind your drill press. To prevent impeding the levers, mount the upper cleat near the highest likely position of your drill-press table, and mount the lower cleat near the bottom ends of the racks.

3. Screw the racks to the cleats. To position the racks, use the inserted lever assembly as a guide, spacing the racks far enough apart to ensure full contact with the undersides of both levers.

COMMERCIAL DRILL-PRESS TABLES

A variety of drill-press tables are available commercially, should you decide to buy one rather than make one yourself. Better models, like this FasTTrak table, come with a fence that accepts flip stops for repeatable drilling (see the top photo at right).

The fence separates at the center to provide greater chuck clearance when using small bits. It attaches to the T-tracks in the table, which also accept hold-downs (not shown) for securing workpieces to the table. If your drill press has a height-adjustment crank, make a notched subbase to allow for crank clearance (see the bottom photo at right).

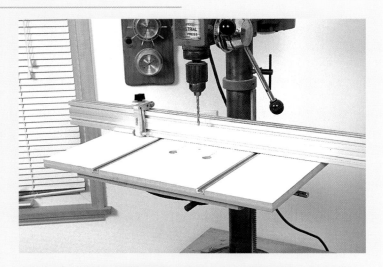

T-TRACK DRILL-PRESS TABLE

FOR A DRILL-PRESS TABLE to be truly useful for woodworking, it needs an adjustable fence and various methods of securing workpieces for drilling. For example, a fence outfitted with stops ensures accurate repeatability when drilling multiple workpieces. And when using a large-diameter bit, a hold-down of some sort is often needed to keep the workpiece from spinning out of control.

Craig Bentzley designed and built this full-featured drill-press table that incorporates T-tracks in both the fence and table. The tracks in the fence accept sliding stops and hold-downs when needed. The tracks in the table also accept hold-downs and provide maximum sliding capacity for the fence. Bentzley incorporated a cutout in the table to accept sacrificial inserts, which minimize exit tearout. An insert can be replaced by pushing it out through the holes in the drill-press table and subtop.

Bentzley built the unit from Baltic birch plywood, plastic laminate, and commercially available hardware. In this section, I've listed the particulars for the parts he used, but similar parts, as well as ready-made commercial fences, are also available from a number of sources (see Sources on p. 172). This table can be customized to suit your needs. If your drill press has a crank that adjusts the table height, you may need to notch out the rear edge of the subtop to allow for the crank swing (see the photo in the sidebar "Commercial Drill-Press Tables" on the facing page). Also, if your metal drill-press table doesn't have a hole in the center, you can either drill one or drill half holes at the edge of the insert cutout to provide finger access (see the drawing "T-Track Drill-Press Table" on p. 84).

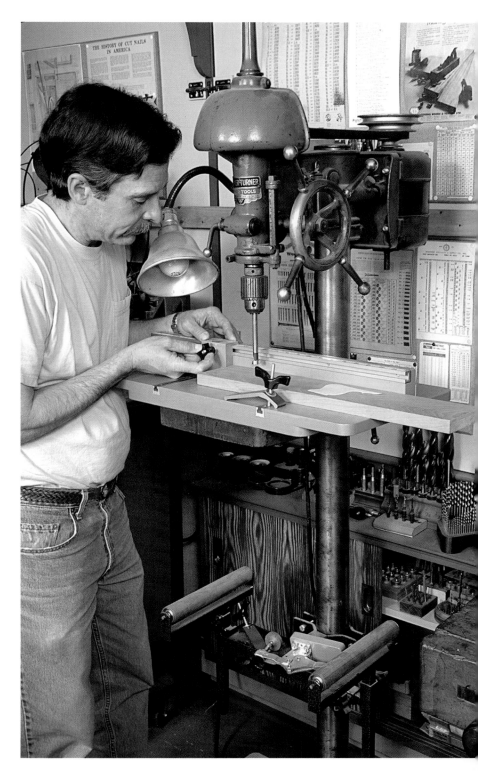

T-Track Drill-Press Table

THE TABLE AND FENCE are each made from two pieces of $3/4$" hardwood plywood. The subtop stiffens the top and serves as the attachment to the metal drill-press table. After slipping the carriage bolts through the subtop, it's attached to the top and then bolted to the metal table.

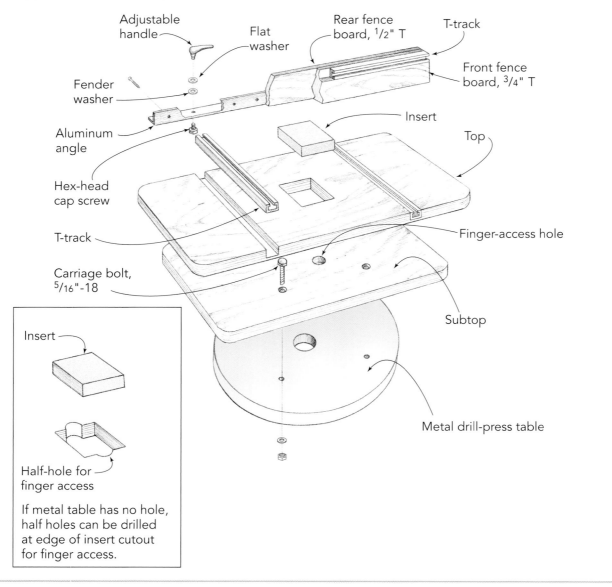

Adjustable handle

Flat washer

Rear fence board, $1/2$" T

T-track

Front fence board, $3/4$" T

Fender washer

Insert

Top

Aluminum angle

Hex-head cap screw

T-track

Finger-access hole

Carriage bolt, $5/16$"-18

Subtop

Metal drill-press table

Insert

Half-hole for finger access

If metal table has no hole, half holes can be drilled at edge of insert cutout for finger access.

Making the Table and Subtop

1. Saw the top and subtop to size. Bentzley's 12-in., front-to-back table depth suits his drill press, but to maximize throat capacity on yours, its depth should extend from the front of your metal table almost to the machine's column. Round the corners of both pieces.

2. Center the subtop side to side on your metal table, and mark for the finger-access hole. Also mark the bolt holes for attachment to the metal tabletop, making sure they avoid any ribs in the metal table.

3. Drill the 1-in.-dia. finger-access hole, and use a Forstner or multispur bit to counterbore the table-attachment bolt holes. Clamp the subtop to the metal table, and drill holes through the subtop and metal table for the attachment bolts.

CUT LIST FOR T-TRACK DRILL-PRESS TABLE

1	Top	¾" x 12" x 24"	Hardwood plywood
1	Base	¾" x 12" x 16"	Hardwood plywood
1	Insert	¾" x 3½" x 3½"	MDF
1	Fence board	¾" x 2¼" x 24"	Hardwood plywood
1	Fence board	½" x 2¼" x 24"	Hardwood plywood

Hardware

2	T-tracks	12" long	From Hartville; part #60706
1	T-track	24" long	From Hartville; part #60716
1	Aluminum angle	⅛" T x 1¼" sq. x 24"	
2	Adjustable handles		From Reid; item #KHA-8
1	Hex-head cap screw	1/4-20 x ¾"	

PHOTO F: After drilling the screw-clearance holes in the T-track, use a ⁹⁄₃₂-in.-dia. twist drill bit to countersink them for #6 flathead screws.

4. Apply plastic laminate to the top, and rout it flush to the edges of the plywood using a flush-trim router bit.

5. Lay the subtop on the top, and trace around the finger-access hole. Mark and cut out the insert opening using a jigsaw. Alternatively, you could rout the cutout using an edge guide. Square up the corners so you won't have to round the corners of your inserts.

6. Cut the dadoes in the top to accept the T-tracks. You can either rout these with a carbide router bit or saw them using a carbide sawblade.

7. Insert the bolts into holes in the subtop, and screw the subtop to the top, making sure to avoid the T-tracks. Paint the edges if you like, and install the whole unit to your metal table. Drill and countersink holes in the T-tracks for #6 flathead screws, and install them into their dadoes (see photo F).

8. Make and install the insert. Better yet, make a bunch of them at once. You'll go through them more quickly than you might think.

Making the Fence

1. Make the two fence boards, cutting them slightly oversize in width and length.

Glue them together, and saw the fence to final size.

2. Apply plastic laminate to the top, front, and back, trimming it flush to the plywood. You can also apply laminate to the ends, or simply paint the ends to match the laminate.

3. Rout or saw the rabbet in the ¾-in.-thick front fence piece, to accept the T-track. Install the track using #6 flathead screws.

4. Cut the aluminum angle to length using a carbide blade. Drill the holes that will attach it to the fence with round-head screws.

5. Lay out the holes for the handle, carefully centering them over the slots in the T-track.

6. Drill the handle holes, and round over sharp corners of the angle with a file.

7. Screw the angle to the fence. Aluminum angles aren't always dead square, so check yours. If necessary, shim between the fence and the angle to square the fence to the table.

8. Install the fence to the table with the handles, using cap screws inside the T-tracks and washers between the handle and the aluminum angle. Use thick washers to ease movement and to prevent the cap screw from bottoming out in the handle. If you like, you can attach a self-adhesive measuring tape to the top edge of the T-track, as Bentzley did.

TIP

When building projects using commercial hardware and fittings, order the parts first to ensure proper fitting and sizing.

This serious (but smiling) turner has everything he needs within reach. Mike Callihan's lathe-tool cabinet accommodates all of his turning tools as well as chucks, calipers, tool rests, and other accessories.

LATHE STATIONS

F THERE'S ONE workstation where woodworkers tend to spend concerted blocks of time, it's at the lathe. Whereas you might flit from chopsaw to planer to jointer to table saw, time at the lathe is often spent in long sessions. Because of this, it's important that your lathe workstation be comfortable and organized.

Lathe workstations aren't typically complicated. Aside from the lathe itself, needs are fairly minimal. Basically, you'll want an accessible rack for your turning tools and storage for your faceplates, calipers, and other accessories. Good lighting is crucial, and a comfortable floor mat is a necessity to minimize leg fatigue and to protect against damage to dropped tools. A grinder for sharpening is the last indispensable item, although it's also handy to have a small table or bench nearby as a staging platform for sandpaper, drills, and other items.

In this chapter, you'll find plans for two wall-hung lathe-tool racks. The racks were designed to hold a lot of tools but can easily be modified to suit your own particular arsenal of gouges, skews, and parting tools. In addition, the sidebars in this chapter show some ideas for making smaller racks, as well as a freestanding combination tool rack/grinder stand. If you like, you can combine any of these ideas to design your own custom solutions. Just remember when designing any sort of workshop project that it's best to first gather all of the intended contents and make sure there's a place for everything. Then incorporate space for future acquisitions.

One last piece of advice, which is offered by many turners, is to make sure you have enough electrical outlets nearby to power your task lights, hand drills, and sanders. Extension cords can trip you up at the lathe and are subject to damage from fumbled tools. If you install new wall outlets, place them about 4 ft. high for better access and use with short tool cords.

CALLIHAN LATHE-
TOOL CABINET

MIKE CALLIHAN HAS acquired quite a few turning tools over the years. When building his new shop, he took the opportunity to make the perfect cabinet for them. The cabinet incorporates several two-piece racks, which each consist of a top piece that is notched to cradle the tool ferrule or shank and a base that's drilled out to accept the butts of the tools. The rack tops are set back from the bases, allowing

the standing tools to lean backward about 10 degrees.

Callihan turns most of his own tool handles, making them the same length and shape. As a result, he was able to position a single notched rack to neatly cradle most of the ferrules in a row. But that's not necessary. If your tool handles are all of differing lengths, the tool shank can rest in the notch just as well. To accommodate widely differing

Callihan Lathe-Tool Cabinet

NOTCHED RACKS support the top ends of tools, and drilled racks hold the butts of the tools. Tools of similar length can be cradled in full-length notched racks supported by cleats on the cabinet sides. To accommodate tools of different lengths in the same cabinet section, shorter runs of notched rack are attached to the cabinet back and side. Cabinet compartments with doors hold lathe chucks and other small accessories.

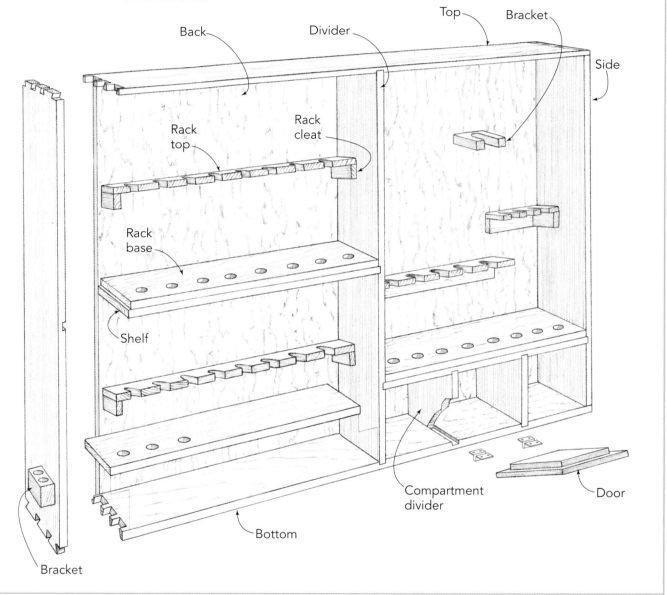

handle lengths in the same cabinet section, the notched racks can be mounted in shorter sections at different heights, as seen in the right side of this cabinet.

The ½-in.-thick back provides enough material for screwing on custom brackets and holders for tool rests, calipers, and other items. The compartments at the lower right house small chucks and other accessories behind hinged doors that flip downward. As a finishing touch, holes drilled at a slight upward angle into the front edges of the cabinet hold pencils and chuck keys.

Using the drawing "Callihan Lathe-Tool Cabinet" above as a reference, you can resize the cabinet to suit your needs. You can easily

CUT LIST FOR CALLIHAN LATHE-TOOL CABINET

2	Sides	¾" x 6" x 42½"	Solid wood
2	Tops/bottoms	¾" x 6" x 61½"	Solid wood
1	Divider	¾" x 5½" x 41¾"	Solid wood
1	Shelf	¾" x 5½" x 30⅜"	Solid wood
1	Back	½" x 60¾" x 41¾"	Hardwood plywood
1	Compartment top	¾" x 5½" x 30⅜"	Solid wood
2	Compartment dividers	¾" x 5½" x 6⅞"	Solid wood
3	Rack tops	¾" x 3" x 29⅝"	Solid wood
3	Rack bases	¾" x 5½" x 29⅝"	Solid wood
6	Rack-side cleats	¾" x 1" x 3³⁄₁₆"	Solid wood
3	Doors	¾" x 6⅝" x 9⅞"	Hardwood plywood

alter the height and width, but keep the depth the same. See the sidebar "Modifying the Cabinets" below for suggestions on how to customize this cabinet for your tools. Callihan decided that joining the corners was a good opportunity to practice his hand-cut dovetail skills, but you could join your corners instead with rabbet-and-dado joints, biscuits, screws, or some other joint.

Making the Pieces and Cutting the Joints

1. Lay out and saw the sides, top, bottom, dividers, and shelves to size. If you're using a corner joint other than dovetails, remember to adjust the length of the case top and bottom to suit the joint.

2. Lay out and cut whatever type of corner joints you've chosen to use. Callihan cut a four-pin dovetail joint at each corner of his cabinet.

3. If you're going to smooth the interior parts and surfaces by sanding or handplaning, do it now. After assembly, the interior

MODIFYING THE CABINETS

Making a lathe-tool cabinet like either one in this chapter offers a great exercise in design modification. Although you could make the projects exactly as shown, you may want to alter them to suit your particular needs. It's not difficult if you follow just a few simple steps.

1. Measure the available wall area for the cabinet, making sure that the unit will span at least two wall studs.

2. On a piece of plywood, apply masking tape to frame an area approximately the size of your allotted wall space.

3. Lay out your turning tools and lathe accessories within the space. Group tools by common length. Allowing a certain amount of space for future acquisitions, play with the groupings. Remember that you can mount brackets on the sides and bottom of a cabinet to hold a single tool or several tools.

4. Once you've determined the size and configuration of the cabinet, make a sketch that includes the measurements and joints. From that, make a cut list of the pieces you'll need. For the cabinet back, use material thick enough to accept nails, pegs, and screws for brackets.

surfaces will be more difficult to sand and virtually impossible to plane. In any case, don't plane or sand the unassembled pieces after cutting the dadoes, or you'll end up with sloppy joint fits.

4. Lay out the ¾-in.-wide dadoes in the sides to accept the shelves. Also, lay out the dadoes for the main divider and compartment dividers.

5. Cut the dadoes to a depth of ⅜ in. You can rout them or saw them on the table saw using a dado head. Guide the workpieces over the dado head using either a crosscut sled or a miter gauge with a long auxiliary fence (see photo A).

6. Saw or rout the ⅜-in. by ½-in. rabbet in the rear edges of the sides, top, and bottom to accept the cabinet back (see the drawing "Callihan Cabinet" at right). Remember to stop short of cutting through corner dovetail joints.

Assembling the Case

For the nicest look, glue and clamp the case. If you're going to paint the cabinet, or if you're going for that strictly utilitarian look, you could more quickly glue and nail or screw it together instead.

1. Dry-assemble the pieces to ensure that the joints fit and to rehearse your assembly procedures. Dry-clamp the sides to the top and bottom, and make the back, fitting it snugly into its rabbets.

2. Glue the divider to the top and bottom. Although you can use clamps, this is a good application for screws because you'll probably never see them anyway. You can insert the back unglued into its rabbets to hold the case square while the glue cures.

3. Assemble the compartment by first inserting the dividers into their dadoes in the case bottom. Then attach the compartment top. There's no harm in screwing the compartment top to the dividers because the screws will be covered by the rack base later.

4. Attach the sides and shelves. Again, insert the back unglued to hold the assembly square while the glue cures.

PHOTO A: You can cut the dadoes for the shelves and divider using a dado head on the table saw. Guide the workpieces using a crosscut sled or a miter gauge with a long auxiliary fence.

Callihan Cabinet
Side View (with side removed)

1"

10°

Suit to tool length.

1/4"

Back 3/4"-thick

Tool-handle hole

Rack top

Rack cleat

Rack bottom

3/8"

1/2"

TIP

When working from plans, don't worry about duplicating the exact spacing and angles of dovetails. Vary them as you like. If you haven't cut dovetails before, you can find instructions for making the joint in a hundred different magazine articles and books.

A SIMPLE WALL RACK

If you don't have a lot of turning tools, a small wall rack may suit your needs. Fred Matlack devised one that consists of nothing more than a couple of notched boards glued to a piece of plywood.

5. After the glue cures, nail the back into its rabbets.

Making the Racks

1. Cut the pieces for each rack, and saw a 10-degree bevel on the rear edge of the rack tops (see the drawing "Callihan Cabinet Side View" on p. 91). While you're at it, make the cleats for mounting the rack tops to the case. Note that the rear end of each cleat is cross-cut at 10 degrees.

2. Mark each rack base for the holes that will accept the butts of the tools. The diameters of the holes can vary to suit handles of different sizes, but keep the front of each hole about ¼ in. from the front of the base. Allow enough space between holes to easily grab the handle.

3. Extend the hole centerlines from each base blank onto its upper mate, and lay out the notches. Callihan found that a 1-in.-wide notch accommodated most of his tools, but some had to be made larger.

4. Drill the holes in the rack bases. A Forstner or multispur bit will give you the cleanest cut. Afterward, rout the top edge of

the hole with a ¼-in. roundover bit to ease insertion of the handles.

5. Cut the notches in the rack tops by first drilling the holes, then sawing inward from the front edge of the piece tangent to the hole diameters. You can make the sawcuts with a jigsaw, with a bandsaw, or by feeding the workpiece on edge over the table-saw blade set to the proper height (see photo B on the facing page). Afterward, ease all sharp corners and edges with sandpaper or rout them with a small roundover bit.

6. Screw the rack cleats to the case, and nail or screw the rack tops to the cleats. Install each rack base with a couple of finish nails.

7. Make the doors from ¾-in.-thick hardwood plywood, and rout a ⅜-in.-wide rabbet around the edges. Install the doors using half-overlay hinges.

8. Make any other special mounts or brackets that you need, and attach them to the case.

9. You can finish up by giving everything a light sanding and a coat or two of oil to protect it from grime.

PHOTO B: To cut the notches in the rack top, first drill the proper-size hole, then saw inward from the edge of the workpiece. The table saw will give you the quickest, straightest cut.

A BED RACK AND TASK-LIGHT BASE

Even if you have a lot of lathe tools, you're often using only a few at a time. You can keep them right at hand on a minirack that rides on the lathe bed. Craig Bentzley's bed rack includes a guide board and magnets attached to the bottom to hold the rack in place (see the top photo). A similarly configured base for a swing-arm lamp allows for versatile task lighting (see the bottom photo).

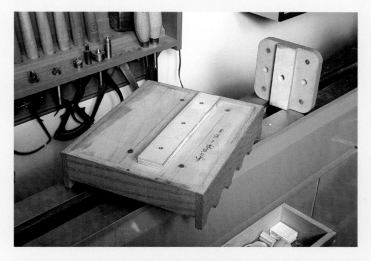

BENTZLEY LATHE-TOOL CABINET

CRAIG BENTZLEY is known for his finely crafted shop as well as his finely crafted furniture. His woodworking skills are reflected in his shop cabinets, fixtures, and racks—all of which are masterfully designed to be both functional and attractive.

This lathe-tool cabinet is a good example of his design approach. At its core, the unit is basically an open cabinet with a shelf. But check out the details. For starters, the coves at the bottoms of the sides provide a lovely transitional element back to the wall. The frame-and-panel back provides a wide, thick frame for attaching the pegs and corbels. The ogee routed on the front edge of the rack bases complements the cabinet's moldings, and the crown molding adds a touch of distinction. Although the corbels provide a bit of support, they're primarily decorative and are meant to visually play off of the curves at the bottoms of the sides. A two-tone paint job highlights the back panels, moldings, and bases. For a trick touch, Bentzley added a steel strip to the front edge of the shelf before painting the cabinet, resulting in a "wood" shelf that holds magnets for posting notes (see photo C on p. 97).

Bentzley made his cabinet from inexpensive pine boards and some scrap plywood. The pegs and moldings were leftovers from previous jobs. You can easily modify the height and width of the cabinet to suit your needs (see the sidebar "Modifying the Cabinets" on p. 90).

Bentzley Lathe-Tool Cabinet

THE CASE IS ASSEMBLED with simple dado joints, which are nailed and glued. The extended sides and filler board at the top provide backing for the crown molding, which is supported by backer blocks. The frame-and-panel back is constructed with tongue-and-groove joinery and is glued into rabbets cut in the rear edges of the cabinet sides.

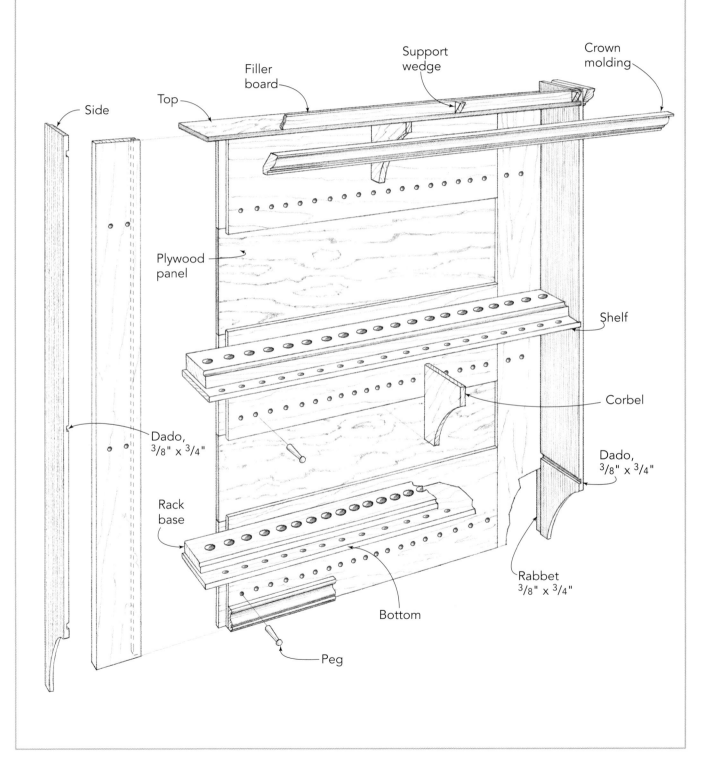

Side

Filler board

Support wedge

Crown molding

Top

Plywood panel

Shelf

Corbel

Dado, 3/8" x 3/4"

Dado, 3/8" x 3/4"

Rack base

Rabbet 3/8" x 3/4"

Bottom

Peg

CUT LIST FOR BENTZLEY LATHE-TOOL CABINET			
1	Top	¾" x 6½" x 45¾"	Solid wood
2	Shelves/bottoms	¾" x 5¾" x 45¾"	Solid wood
2	Sides	¾" x 6½" x 52"	Solid wood
1	Filler board	¾" x 45" x (*see note)	Solid wood
2	Rack bases	1⅛" x 3½" x 45"	Solid wood
2	Corbels	¾" x 4½" x 4½"	Solid wood
2	Stiles	¾" x 5⅜" x 49"	Solid wood
1	Top rail**	¾" x 11¼" x 36"	Solid wood
1	Center rail **	¾" x 11" x 36"	Solid wood
1	Bottom rail**	¾" x 9½" x 36"	Solid wood
1	Top panel	¼" x 36" x 6¼"	Plywood
1	Bottom panel	¼" x 36" x 13"	Plywood
	Moldings	To suit	
	Pegs	To suit	

*Suit to match height of chosen crown molding.
** Length of rails includes tongues.

Cove

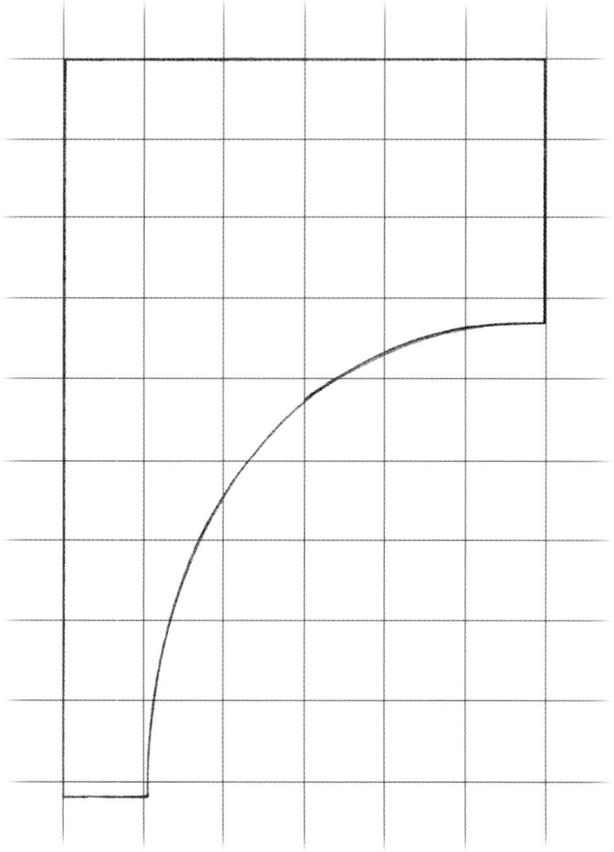

Making the Case Parts

1. Cut the sides, top, bottom, shelf, and rack bases to size. Lay out the coves at the bottom of the sides (see the drawing "Cove" below).

2. Lay out and rout or saw the ⅜-in. by ¾-in. dadoes in the sides. Locate the upper dadoes by determining the installed height of your chosen crown molding, which should be even with the top ends of the sides.

3. Cut the ⅜-in. by ¾-in. rabbets in the rear edges of the sides, and use a jigsaw to cut the curves on the bottom edges of the sides (see photo D on p. 98).

4. Drill holes in the front edges of the shelf and case bottom to accommodate current tools and future acquisitions. Bentzley varied the diameters of his holes from ⅝ in. to 1⅛ in.

5. Lay out the holes in the rack bases to accept your turning tools' handles. Bentzley spaced his 1¼-in.-dia. holes about ½ in. apart. Strike a line at the rear edge of the base to mark the midpoint between holes. You'll use these lines later as a reference when laying out the peg holes on the back.

Making the Back and Drilling the Rack Holes

1. Cut to size the rails and stiles for the back. Saw or rout a ¼-in.-wide by ½-in.-deep groove into the edges of the pieces as shown in the drawing "Frame-and-Panel Back" on the facing page.

2. On the ends of each rail, saw two opposing rabbets to create a centered tongue that fits snugly into the grooves in the stiles.

3. Saw the ¼-in.-thick plywood panels to size. Dry-assemble the whole back to ensure that the tongue-and-groove joints fit well and that the plywood panels are the proper size.

4. Strike a horizontal line along each rail to locate the intended row of pegs.

PHOTO C: Wooden pegs keep the standing tool shanks separated while different-size holes drilled through the front of the shelves accommodate turning tools as well as drive centers and other accessories. Magnets curiously stick to the front of the shelf, which includes an attached metal strip under its painted surface.

TIP

To prevent assemblies from buckling under clamp pressure, make sure that the clamp screws are centered across the thickness of the stock.

5. Center each rack base in position on the dry-assembled back, and transfer the midpoint marks you made earlier onto the frame rails. Use a framing square to transfer the location of each mark upward to the horizontal line at the peg-row location. Also, lay out your chosen peg-hole spacing across the bottom rail.

6. Disassemble the back and drill the peg holes, using a drill press to ensure that they are square to the face of the back. Alternatively, you could drill the holes using a portable drill guide or a squarely drilled block clamped to the rail.

7. Using a Forstner or multispur bit, drill the holes in the rack bases, stopping short of the bottom by ⅛ in. (see photo E on p. 98).

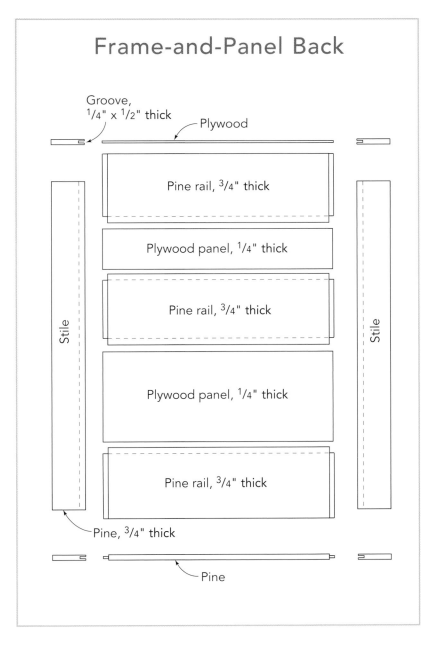

Frame-and-Panel Back

Groove, ¼" x ½" thick

Plywood

Pine rail, ¾" thick

Plywood panel, ¼" thick

Pine rail, ¾" thick

Plywood panel, ¼" thick

Pine rail, ¾" thick

Stile

Stile

Pine, ¾" thick

Pine

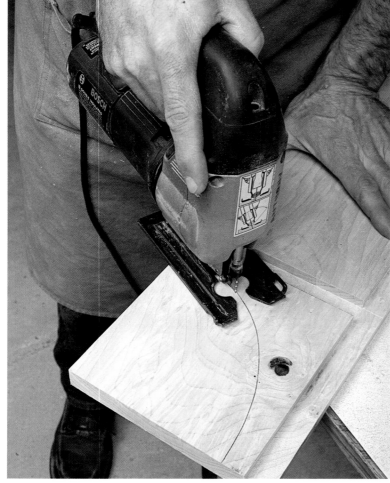

PHOTO D: Cut the curves on the bottom edges of the sides after sawing the dadoes for the bottom shelf and the rabbet for the back.

PHOTO E: Use a Forstner or multispur bit to drill flat-bottom holes in the rack bases, stopping short of the bottom by ⅛ in.

Assembling the Cabinet

1. Glue up the back, making sure that the assembly is flat and square under clamp pressure. After the glue cures, sand or plane the joints flush.

2. Dry-clamp the case together. Trim the edges of the frame-and-panel assembly as necessary to fit snugly between the rabbets at the rear edges of the sides.

3. Glue and nail the sides to the top, bottom, and shelf, and glue and nail the back into its rabbets. Screw down through the cabinet top into the upper back rail.

4. Glue the pegs into their holes.

5. Make and attach the corbels, screwing them in place through the cabinet back.

6. Fit the crown molding to the top of the cabinet, tacking it in place with brads. Cut a few wedges as shown in the drawing "Bentzley Lathe-Tool Cabinet" on p. 95 and glue them into place behind the molding to help support it.

7. Putty any nail holes, give everything a light sanding, and paint the cabinet. At the same time, paint the rack bases and the moldings that will cover the screws after installation.

8. Attach the rack bases, tacking them in place through the bottom of a couple of holes.

9. Hang the cabinet, and install the moldings that hide the screws. Job well done.

A TOOL RACK/GRINDER STAND

Walt Segl decided to consolidate his tool rack and grinder stand into one package. He designed and built a cabinet with a rotating top to serve his purposes. The base cabinet stores lathe tool accessories, while the top carries his grinder and turning tools (see the bottom photo at left).

Stepped holes in the top accept a variety of turning tools while turned pegs inset into the sides of the top allow hanging of calipers (see the bottom photo at right). The top rotates around its center bolt while gliding on thin strips of polyethylene plastic tape attached to the cabinet top.

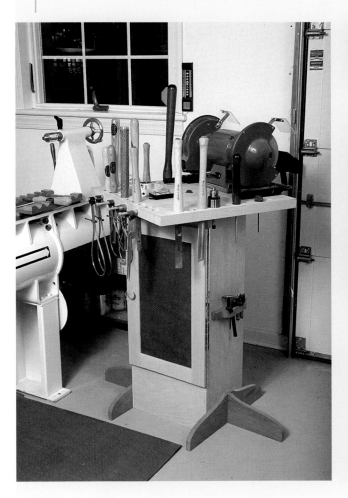

The author's chopsaw cabinet is deep enough to house lumber and panel offcuts and includes extension tables with flip stops for accurate, repetitive cutting.

CHOPSAW CABINET WITH EXTENSION TABLES

THE POWER MITER SAW, also called a chop saw, has become a real mainstay in the woodshop over the last 20 years or so—particularly the sliding compound miter (SCM) saw, which rides on a rail or rails, allowing wider crosscuts, miters, and bevels than a standard miter saw. Because of its length of travel, an SCM saw requires a fairly deep (front-to-back) surface to sit on. Therefore, it makes sense to build a deep cabinet that will support the saw well and also provide storage for large shop supplies.

A deep cabinet also provides the perfect opportunity to house panel offcuts and lumber shorts that otherwise litter a shop. I designed this cabinet with narrow end sections for those uses and a bank of large drawers down the center to store coffee cans full of hardware. The top is a 6-ft. length of second-hand wooden countertop. The 16-in.-wide overhang on the left provides a space for a shop vacuum. I used birch plywood for the case and maple for the face frame and drawer fronts. The drawer boxes are poplar.

To provide support at the sides of the saw, you can use simple riser blocks or even an adjacent work surface (see the sidebar "Neighboring Workpiece Support" on p. 103). However, extension tables with an integral fence are a much better approach. Simple boxed forms can sometimes fit the bill (see the photo in the sidebar "Basic Extension Tables" on p. 117). However, I decided to outfit my fences with slotted aluminum track that accepts flip stops for efficient production (see the sidebar "Flip Stops" on p. 117). The fences bolt to the tables through fender-washer shims, creating a ⅛-in.-wide chute for dust and chips. The table overhang at the front serves as a clamping ledge when necessary.

My shop doesn't allow room for long, fixed extension tables, so I designed a telescoping arm that rides inside the left-hand table (see the drawing "Extension Table with Telescoping Arm" on p. 115). When the arm is extended 2 ft., I have 6 ft. to the left of the blade, meaning I can load 12-ft.-long boards without them tipping. When not in use, the arm is tucked away, preserving precious wall space.

CHOPSAW CABINET

THE HARDWOOD PLYWOOD CASE is constructed with dado joints and rabbet joints. The top and bottom are glued and screwed to the dividers. The sides are glued and nailed to the top and bottom. The face frame is joined with loose tenons, then glued and nailed to the plywood case. The kick plate extends up to the case bottom to provide extra support for heavy loads.

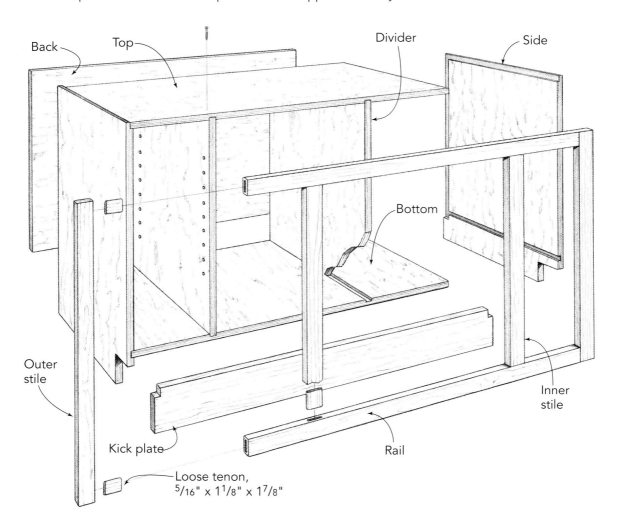

Back · Top · Divider · Side · Bottom · Outer stile · Inner stile · Kick plate · Rail · Loose tenon, 5/16" x 1 1/8" x 1 7/8"

THE BIRCH PLYWOOD cabinet is built using standard face-frame construction. The ½-in.-thick back provides better rigidity than a ¼-in.-thick back and won't crack if you slam stored plywood offcuts against it. Note that the drawer boxes are installed in the case before attaching the case to the wall. The drawer fronts are attached afterward.

Building the Case

Cutting the parts and joints

1. Lay out the plywood pieces and saw them to size. Leave the shelves slightly oversize in width for now. It's best to fit them snugly between the shelf clips after case assembly.

2. Mark the edges of the pieces for orientation. I use the triangle marking system (see the drawing on p. 14).

3. Saw or rout the dadoes in the sides to accept the bottom (see the sidebar "Fitting Dado Joints in Plywood"on p. 104). Because nominal ¾-in.-thick hardwood plywood is really less than ¾ in. thick, lay out the joint so its upper edge is 5¾ in. from the bottom edge of the side (see the drawing "Elevations" on p. 104). I cut the joints on the table saw, registering the ends of the panels against the rip fence.

4. Lay out and cut the dadoes in the top and bottom to accept the sides. If handling panels this large on the table saw feels awkward, rout the joints using a straight edge instead.

Assembling the plywood case

1. Dry-assemble the case to check the joint fits and to rehearse your assembly procedures. Using a square and light pencil lines, lay out the nail and screw paths for the joints.

2. Glue and screw the top and bottom to the dividers.

3. Use glue and #6 finish nails to attach the sides to the top and bottom (see photo A on p. 105). If your case pieces vary somewhat in width, align the back edges because the back rabbets impede plane travel, which prevents planing or sanding the joints flush after assembly. Dry-clamp the back in place to hold the case square while the glue cures.

CUT LIST FOR CHOPSAW CABINET

2	Sides	¾" x 27¼" x 34¼"	Hardwood plywood
2	Dividers	¾" x 26¾" x 28½"	Hardwood plywood
2	Tops/ bottoms	¾" x 26¾" x 53¼"	Hardwood plywood
1	Back	½" x 29¼" x 53¼"	Hardwood plywood
2	Stiles	¾" x 1¾" x 30¼"	Solid wood
2	Stiles	¾" x 1¾" x 26¾"	Solid wood
2	Rails	¾" x 1¾" x 50½"	Solid wood
1	Top	1¾" x 25" x 72"	Solid wood
3	Shelves	¾" x 26½" x 13¼"	Hardwood plywood
1	Kick plate	¾" x 4" x 54"	Solid wood
Drawers			
3	Fronts	¾" x 8⅞" x 24"	Solid wood
6	Sides	⅝" x 7⅞" x 25 5/16"	Solid wood
6	Fronts/ backs	⅝" x 7⅞" x 23"	Solid wood
3	Bottoms	½" x 25½" x 22¼"	Hardwood plywood
Hardware			
3 pairs	Drawer slides	26" full extension	Woodworker's Hardware, item # KV8417 B26

NEIGHBORING WORKPIECE SUPPORT

Walt Segl's portable chopsaw cart does not accommodate extension tables. Instead, when he needs to crosscut long boards, he rolls the cart next to his workbench for support. A panel resting under the board on the workbench raises the workpiece to the saw-table height.

Elevations

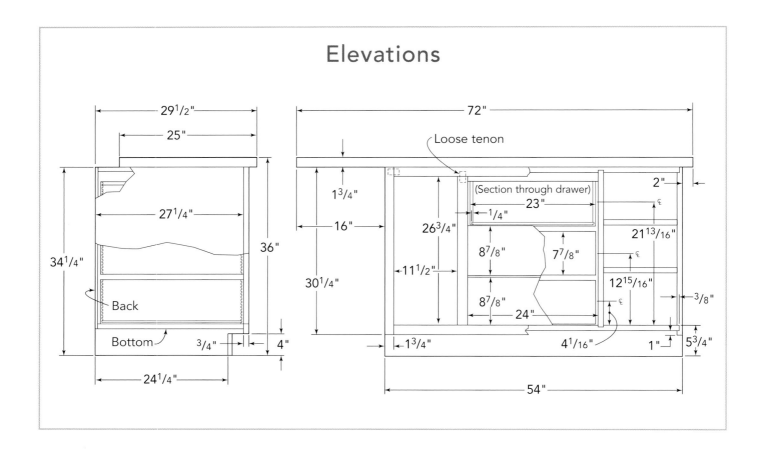

FITTING DADO JOINTS IN PLYWOOD

Cutting dadoes to join plywood panels can be a bit tricky. Even good-quality hardwood plywood can vary in thickness across the sheet, resulting in erratic fits along the length of a joint. However, I like my dadoes to fit snugly to prevent joint gaps and to help hold the case together during dry-fitting. Here's how I approach it.

Using dial calipers or a finely graduated ruler, I measure the thickness of the panel edges to be inserted in the joints. I set up a dado head on my table saw to the width of the thinnest area. Test-cutting in scrap, I shim the head to create a dado that's about 0.002-in. wider than the thinnest edge.

To fit each panel into its dado, I thin down the fat sections using a belt sander fitted with a 120-grit belt. Rather than risking sand-through on one face, I split the loss, sanding a bit off of both faces. When sanding, take care to keep the sander platen flat on the work, particularly as you partially suspend it off the end of the panel.

I'll admit that some of my woodworking pals consider this fussy. Like them, you may be perfectly happy with slightly gapped joints that are quicker to make.

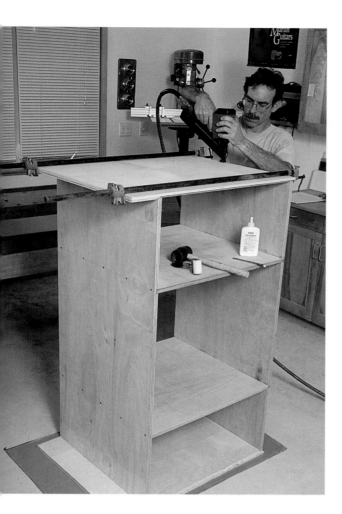

PHOTO A: Pipe clamps are used to pull the case top against its rabbet shoulder while gluing and nailing the sides to the top and bottom. The clamps are removed immediately after nailing.

DUAL-LEVEL SAWS

Bob Whitley cantilevered his chopsaw out over his radial-arm saw table, conserving shop space and consolidating his crosscutting capabilities into a compact area.

Making and attaching the face frame

I used loose tenons for the face-frame joinery, but you could use mortise-and-tenon joints, pocket screws, dowels, or biscuits.

1. Make the rails and stiles, but rip the outer stiles about ½2 in. oversize in width. You'll trim the resulting overhang flush to the sides after attaching the face frame to the plywood case. While you're at it, make extra stock for tool setup.

2. Using the divider spacing for reference, lay out the inner-stile joints, marking the intersection of each stile edge fully across the edge of each rail. Position each stile so that its innermost edge will slightly overhang its divider.

3. Rout the ⅜-in.-wide by 1¼-in.-long by 1-in.-deep mortises for all the joints. I use a shopmade jig for this (see the sidebar "Router Mortising Jig" on pp. 106–7).

ROUTER MORTISING JIG

In a typical "loose tenon" joint, a mortise is routed into the edge of one member (in this case the stile) and a mating mortise is routed into the end of the other member (here, the rail). A separately made tenon is then glued into the mortises to create a very strong joint.

Edge mortises are easy to rout using a standard router edge guide. However, end mortises require a jig to hold the workpiece vertical and provide router support. The mortising jig shown here allows the routing of edge mortises and end mortises with the same edge-guide setting. Router-travel stops ensure mortises of matching length. The vertical fence can be installed at an angle for routing mortises in the ends of mitered pieces. Here's how the jig works to cut face frame joints:

1. Mark the rail spacing on the inner edges of your face-frame stiles. Then lay out one stile mortise.

2. Install an upcut spiral bit of the proper diameter in your router.

3. Clamp the stile to the jig with the stile's inner edge aligned with the top edge of the jig. (Important: To ensure flush joints, always place the inner face of a workpiece against the face of the jig.) Align the rail position mark (or end of the stile when appropriate) with a line drawn upward from the jig's fence (see the photo above).

4. Adjust your router edge guide to locate the bit over the marked-out mortise. Position the bit at one end of the mortise, and clamp a stop against the appropriate side of the router base. Slide the router to the opposite end of the mortise, and clamp the other stop in place.

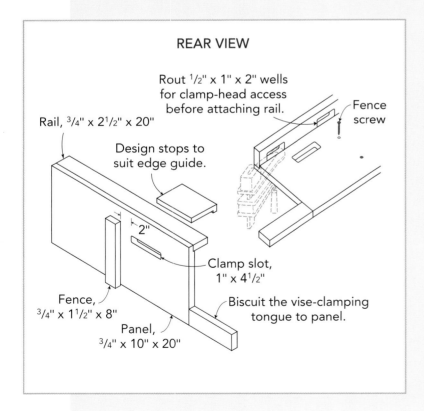

REAR VIEW

Rout 1/2" x 1" x 2" wells for clamp-head access before attaching rail.

Fence screw

Rail, 3/4" x 2 1/2" x 20"

Design stops to suit edge guide.

2"

Clamp slot, 1" x 4 1/2"

Fence, 3/4" x 1 1/2" x 8"

Biscuit the vise-clamping tongue to panel.

Panel, 3/4" x 10" x 20"

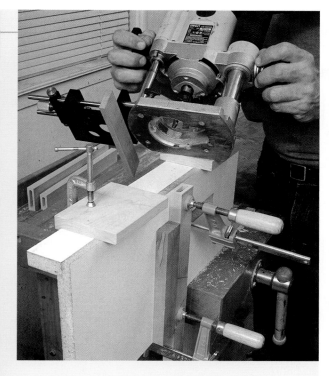

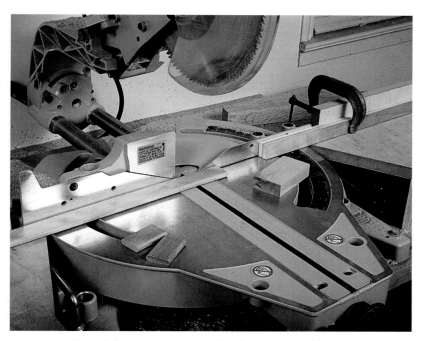

PHOTO B: To safely crosscut multiple short pieces like these loose tenons, set the cutup using a spacer placed against the stop block. Remove the spacer before making each cut.

5. Rout the mortise in successive passes, pushing the router away from you with the edge guide to your right. Maintain firm downward pressure on the half of the router that rides on the jig.

6. Rout all other stile mortises of the same length in the same manner.

7. To set up to rout the mating mortises, clamp a rail in place against the jig's fence, and flush to the top of the jig (see the photo above). Without changing the position of the stops, rout the mortise. Repeat for all other rail mortises of the same length.

8. To rout mortises of a different length, simply adjust the position of the right-hand stop, then rout the matching stile and rail mortises in the same manner as above.

This process reads more complicated than it is. Once you've completed one set of joints using this jig, you'll find the process very efficient.

4. Mill a length of ⁵⁄₁₆-in.-thick by 1⅛-in.-wide loose tenon stock. Rout, sand, or plane a bullnose profile on the edges of the stock, and cut the pieces to 1⅞ in. long. You can do this safely on the chopsaw using a spacer block (see photo B).

5. Glue up the face frame making sure it's flat and square under clamp pressure (see photos C and D on p. 108).

6. Plane or sand the face-frame joints flush on both faces. Also, sand or plane the plywood case joints flush if necessary.

7. With the case lying on its back, compare the diagonal corner measurements to make sure everything is square. Sight across the cabinet's front edges to make sure the case is flat; shim the corners if necessary. Attach the face frame using glue and nails.

8. After the glue cures, trim any frame overlaps flush to the plywood. I use a flush-trim bit in a laminate trimmer (see photo E on p. 109).

9. Mark and cut out the kick-plate notch in each case side using a jigsaw.

TIP

When gluing up, I use a clean, damp rag to quickly wipe glue squeeze-out from each joint as I pull it together. Glue wipes away much easier when it's fresh and wet. Refresh your cleanup water regularly to prevent wiping diluted glue into the wood pores.

PHOTO C: After performing a dry-assembly, glue up the face frame on a flat surface. Lay everything out in an orderly fashion, with all preset clamps close at hand.

PHOTO D: To prevent buckling under clamp pressure, use ¾-in.-dia. dowels to center the pressure against the edges of the ¾-in.-thick stock. Sight down each clamp to make sure it's centered across the width of the workpiece.

PHOTO E: Rout the face-frame overlap using a flush-trim bit.

PHOTO F: When puttying nail holes, load just a dab of putty on the corner of the knife to minimize the spreading of the putty into adjacent wood pores.

10. Make and fit the kick plate. It extends 5 in. up to provide support against the case bottom, so you'll need to notch it at the ends (see the drawing "Chopsaw Cabinet" on p. 102). Cut it close to the exact length, as any overlap will have to be planed or sanded flush to the case side. Glue and nail the kick plate to the sides.

11. Putty the nail holes, applying the putty judiciously (see photo F). Finish-sand the cabinet.

12. Drill shelf-pin holes in the end sections (see photo G).

13. At this point, I suggest applying a coat of wiping varnish to the cabinet so the finish can dry while you work on the drawers. Apply the second coat later.

Making and Installing the Drawers

These large drawers need to be strong, so I joined them with ½-in. half-blind dovetails that I cut on a commercial jig. However, you could use a routed drawer lock joint instead (see the sidebar "Routed Drawer Lock Joint"

PHOTO G: A plywood template is used to establish the shelf-pin spacing. A dowel on the drill bit serves as a depth stop.

Drawer

LARGE DRAWERS need strong joints. These drawers were joined at the corners with jig-cut half-blind dovetails. The $1/2$"-thick plywood bottom is rabbeted on the underside to slip into its $1/4$" x $1/4$" grooves. To prevent exposing the grooves, they should run through the tails and sockets as shown, rather than through the pins.

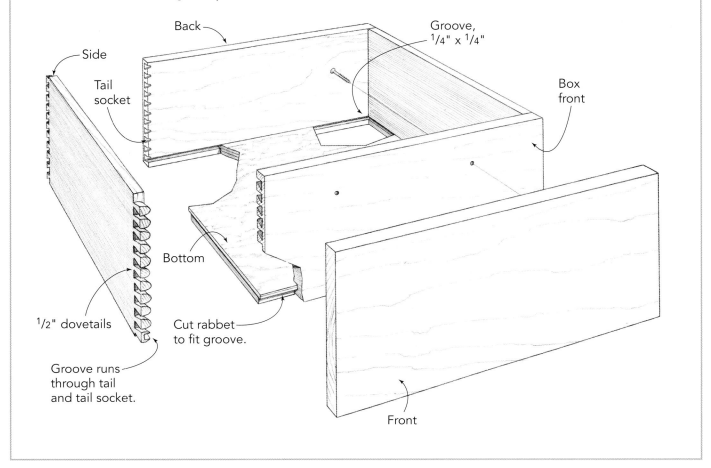

Back

Groove,
$1/4$" x $1/4$"

Side

Tail
socket

Box
front

$1/2$" dovetails

Bottom

Cut rabbet
to fit groove.

Groove runs
through tail
and tail socket.

Front

on pp. 154–55). Whatever kind of joint you use, remember that the finished drawer needs to be 1 in. narrower than the case opening to accommodate the commercial drawer slides.

Building the boxes

1. If you're using a different kind of joint than ½-in. half-blind dovetails, make a cut list of the necessary parts.

2. Make the parts for the boxes. Accurate sawing here makes a big difference in the fit and installation of the drawers, so work carefully. You can make the drawer fronts now, too, but leave them at least ¼ in. oversize in

width and length for now. You'll trim them to fit later.

3. Mark the parts for orientation, and cut the joints. Notice that the drawer-bottom groove runs through the tails, not the pins (see the drawing "Drawer" above). If it ran through the pins, the groove would expose itself at the drawer sides.

4. Dry-clamp to make sure all the parts fit well, then glue up the drawer boxes on a flat surface. I just spot-glue the bottoms, applying a couple of dabs of glue in each groove.

5. After the glue cures, plane or sand the joints flush.

PHOTO H: After determining the drawer-slide spacing, you can make plywood spacers for easy, accurate installation of the slides.

Installing the drawer boxes

Commercial drawer slides typically consist of two parts: one part that attaches to the case and another part that attaches to the drawer box. With the slides that I used, you mount the sliding-rail assembly on the case and a quick-disconnect rail on the drawer box. If you use a different style of slide, refer to its installation instructions.

1. Mark the intended location of each sliding-rail assembly on the case dividers. Calculate the spacing so that the rails will be centered on the drawer-box sides (see the drawing "Elevations" on p. 104). Make the plywood spacers.

2. Screw the lowermost slides to their case dividers. An appropriately sized spacer will ensure that the slides are parallel to the case bottom, thus square to the face frame.

3. Use appropriately sized spacers for installing the center drawer slides (see photo H). You can use the same spacers to install the top slides.

4. Screw the rails to the drawer boxes, centering them halfway up the drawer side (see photo I). For now, install each rail with just two screws through the vertical slots.

PHOTO I: After centering one drawer-half of a slide on a drawer, make a spacer for installing the slides on all of the drawers.

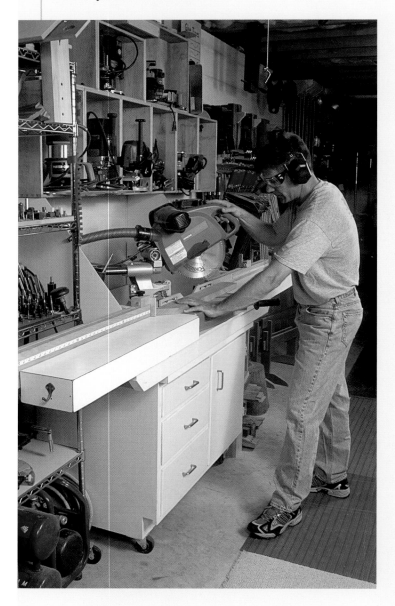

5. Install the drawer boxes, and adjust the rail position on the drawers as necessary to bring the entire front of each drawer box flush with the rear face of the face frame. When everything is aligned properly, install the rest of the screws in the drawer rail holes.

Installing the Case

1. Lay the cabinet on its front on the floor, and sight across the ends to make sure the rear edges are in the same plane. If necessary, shim the corners. Glue and nail the cabinet back into its rabbets.

2. Fit the cabinet in place, and check it for level. If the floor is tilted or seriously uneven, you need to either shim the cabinet or else scribe and trim its bottom edges to accommodate floor irregularities.

3. Install the cabinet by screwing it to the wall studs through the ½-in.-thick plywood back. If the wall isn't flat, shim the studs as necessary to keep the entire front of the cabinet in the same plane.

Attaching the Drawer Fronts

1. Begin with the front for the bottom drawer, ripping it to 8⅞ in. wide. Before crosscutting it to length, check the square of your case opening. If it's perfectly square, crosscut the drawer front to be ¹⁄₁₆ in. less than the opening. If the opening is not square, crosscut the drawer front so it touches both stiles.

2. Place ¹⁄₁₆-in. shims on the case bottom, and clamp the drawer front to its box. Mark for trimming the ends (see photo J on facing page). Aim for a gap of ³⁄₆₄ in. on each side. Use a sharp block plane to trim the end grain.

3. Reclamp the trimmed drawer front to the box. Remove the box, and drill four countersunk holes through the box to attach the front. Install two screws, remove the clamps, and recheck the fit in the case. If the alignment is fine, install the other screws. If the

PHOTO J: To fit the drawer fronts, shim them for proper spacing and then mark the ends near the corners for a consistent gap, making sure they're parallel with the adjacent stiles. Connect the marks with a fine pencil line run against a straightedge, and plane to the line.

alignment is off, remove the installed screws, adjust the position of the front, and install the other two screws. When everything is aligned, drive home all four screws.

4. Install the center drawer front in the same manner, using shims placed on the top edge of the bottom drawer.

5. To install the top drawer, which doesn't provide clamp access, begin by drilling four ⅛-in.-dia. holes through the box front near the corners. Drive a couple of #6 drywall screws through the bottom holes until the screws project about ⅛ in. Install the drawer box, and

press the shimmed, centered drawer front firmly against the screw tips. Put the drawer on a bench and align the front by locating the screw tips in their depressions (enlarging the depressions with an awl can help).

6. After all the fronts are installed, use a sharp block plane to do any final edge trimming. Ease the sharp edges and corners with 220-grit sandpaper.

7. Finish-sand the fronts, apply finish, and install pulls.

TIP

I often install a cabinet before attaching its drawer fronts. If you install the fronts first, you run the risk of tweaking them out of alignment if the case isn't installed perfectly square.

EXTENSION TABLE
WITH TELESCOPING ARM

It's important to use a strong, stable hardwood like maple for the telescoping arm. To ensure an enduring fit between the arm and the extension table, use the same wood for the rails and the table front and back so they'll expand and contract at the same rate. If you don't plan to install a telescoping arm, you can simply use plywood for the table fronts and backs.

I've provided the cut list for my extension tables, which suit my 72-in.-long cabinet top and my 10-in. Makita® LS1013 saw, with its 4⅜-in.-high table. But unless you have that saw, you'll need to modify the sizes to suit your particular saw and cabinet top, as I'll discuss along the way. The best approach for this particular project is to stick-build the units, sizing the parts one at a time as you go along, as I'll discuss here.

Making the Extension Tables

Making the parts

1. Begin by attaching your saw to the cabinet top using lag screws. (*Important: If your saw has flexible feet, remove them.*) Make certain the chopsaw fence is parallel to the front edge of the cabinet top and that the fully retracted saw carriage rails don't hit the wall. The blade on my saw sits 44 in. from the left-hand end of the table, leaving 28 in. to the right. I favor making the left-hand table longer because that's the side I generally load boards on. Plus, a longer table allows a longer telescoping arm, which will effectively extend the length of its extension table by two-thirds.

2. Rip the ½-in.-thick by 10¾-in.-wide plywood pieces for the bases. To determine the length of each piece, measure away from the

Extension Table with Telescoping Arm

THE TELESCOPING ARM rides inside the extension table. The lock knob draws its bolt against the T-track in the rail to lock the arm at any desired projection. The main fence bolts to the main extension table through slots to allow adjustment for accurately setting the measuring tape in relation to the sawblade.

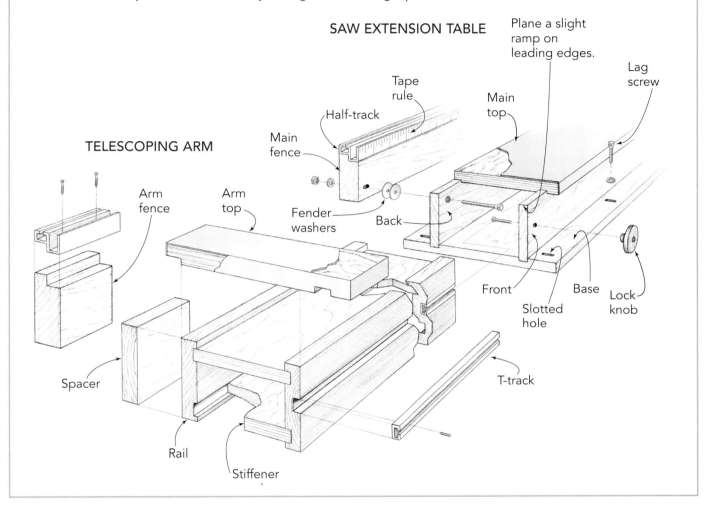

SAW EXTENSION TABLE

TELESCOPING ARM

base of your saw to each end of your cabinet top, and subtract ¼ in.

3. Make the ¾-in.-thick fronts and backs. To determine the width of the pieces, subtract 1 in. from the height of your chopsaw table. Cut the pieces to the same lengths as your bases.

4. Make the 8-in.-wide tops from ¾-in.-thick hardwood plywood or MDF. To determine the length of the right-hand piece, measure over from the top edge of your saw table to the end of the cabinet top, and subtract ¼ in. For the telescoping tabletop, measure to the left-hand end of the cabinet top, and add 2 in.

Laminating the tops

1. Apply plastic laminate to the outer ends, front edges, and tops of the tables. Cut oversize strips and glue them to the edges with contact cement. Rout the strips flush to the plywood with a flush-trim bit.

2. Cut oversize pieces for the tops, and apply them (see photo K on p. 118). Use a hard roller or straight-side glass jar to press the laminate firmly into the cement.

3. Bevel the sharp edges with a mill file (see photo L on p. 118).

Mitering the tops for saw swing

The design of most chopsaws require that the innermost ends of the extension tables be cut away to accommodate the saw-table handle when it's swung over for miter cuts.

1. Cut a length of cardboard into an 8-in.-wide strip. With the saw table rotated fully to one side and with the rear edge of the card-board in the same plane as your saw fence, mark and cut the end of the cardboard to allow full swing of the saw handle. Repeat for the opposite top.

2. Using the cardboard template, transfer the angle to the ends of your tables, and cut the angles.

Cutting the joints and mitering the fronts and bases

1. Cut the ⅛-in.-deep grooves and rabbets in the undersides of the tops (see photo M on p. 118). I sawed them with a dado head on the table saw, but you could rout them instead. Make the joint as snug as possible to ensure a uniform distance between the unit's front and back all along their lengths.

2. Lay out the grooves in the bases to exactly match the spacing of the grooves in the tops. This is important for the ultimate squareness of the units.

3. Set up to cut the grooves in the bases. Make a test cut in ½-in.-thick plywood, then dry-fit the scrap, top, and front together to ensure that the height of the assembled unit will match the height of your saw table. Adjust the depth of the groove as necessary to yield that overall measurement, and cut the grooves in the bases.

4. Dry-assemble the units in place next to your saw. Transfer the angle of the tops onto the top edges of the fronts, and cut the angles on the fronts. Transfer the angles of the fronts onto the bases, and cut them to the same angle. Your saw should now have full swing in both directions.

5. Push or clamp the tables tightly against the cabinet top and use a long, accurate straightedge to ensure that the extension tables are level with your saw table. If they're a bit too high, you can trim the width of the front and back pieces as necessary. If the tables are a bit low, don't worry; you can shim them later during installation.

6. Crosscut 3¼ in. off the end of the left-hand top. This will be the section that you attach to the telescoping rails later.

CUT LIST FOR EXTENSION TABLES

Tables*

1	Top	¾" x 8" x (37¼")	Hardwood plywood
1	Top	¾" x 8" x (19")	Hardwood plywood
1	Bottom	½" x 10¾" x (33¾")	Hardwood plywood
1	Bottom	½" x 10¾" x (17½")	Hardwood plywood
2	Fronts/backs	¾" x (3⅜") x (33¾")	Maple
2	Fronts/backs	¾" x (3⅜") x (17½")	Maple
1	Fence	1⁵⁄₁₆" x 4⅝" x (36")	Maple
1	Fence	1⁵⁄₁₆" x 4⅝" x (18")	Maple

Telescoping Arm*

1	Top	¾" x 8" x 3"	Hardwood plywood
2	Rails	¾" x (3⅛") x (34¾")	Maple
2	Panels	½" x 4½" x (34¾")	Hardwood plywood
1	Fence	1⁵⁄₁₆" x 4⅝" x 3¼"	Maple
1	Spacer	⅞" x (3⅛") x 1⅞"	Maple

Hardware

1	T-track	36"	Woodcraft minitrack, item #128219
1	T-knob	2"	Rockler, item #71506
1	Half-track	18"	From FasTTrak
1	Half-track	36"	From FasTTrak
1	Hex bolt	1½" x ¼"-20	
5	Hex bolts with washers and nuts	⅜" x 2½"	
10	Fender washers	¹⁄₁₆" thick	

*Modify the figures in parentheses to suit the height and lengths of your tables.

Cutting the attachment holes and slots

Before gluing up the extension table, it's necessary to rout the lag-screw slots in the base, drill the hole in the front for the lock knob, and drill and chop the holes for the fence bolts.

1. Mark out and rout the ⁵⁄₁₆-in.-wide by ½-in.-long slots in the base. I spaced them about 1½ in. in from the ends and added centered slots in the long table (see photo N on p. 119).

2. Mark out the lock-knob hole in the front fence, carefully centering it halfway up the front and 1½ in. in from the end. Bore it on the drill press.

3. Mark the fence-attachment bolt holes in the back pieces, setting them in about 2 in. from the ends, with an additional hole in the center of the long table. Locate them ⅝ in. down from the top of the back, as shown in the drawing "End View" on p. 119. Again, bore these on the drill press.

4. Cut the bolt-head recesses in the backs (see photo O on p. 119).

5. The last thing to do before assembly is to sand and wax the inside faces of the top, front, back, and base to minimize friction on the telescoping section. Be careful not to get wax on the surfaces to be glued.

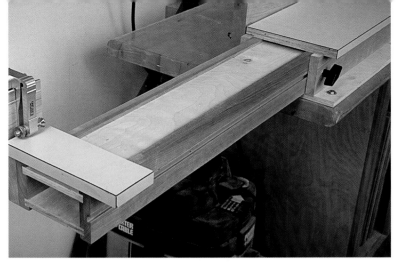

The telescoping arm locks to the extension table and includes an adjustable flip stop for efficient cutting of workpiece multiples.

FLIP STOPS

A flip stop is an efficient device for crosscutting multiple workpieces to the same length. When using a fixed stop to cut multiples, all of the workpieces must be handled twice—first to square the ends, then to cut them to the same length against the stop. However, a flip stop can simply be flipped out of the way for the first cut and then flipped down to make the final cut. A flip stop left in position on the fence is also handy for those occasions when you screw up a workpiece and have to cut a replacement to the same length later.

BASIC EXTENSION TABLES

A quick chopsaw setup can be made by mounting a length of commercial countertop to an available base cabinet. The extension tables shown here were made from scrap plywood and MDF. The back piece extends up past the tabletops to create a fence for supporting stock and a place to clamp stop are screwed to the countertop from underneath.

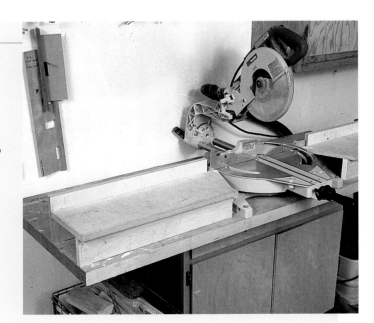

TIP

Plastic-laminate scraps are often available free of charge from commercial cabinet shops. Get a solid, light color if possible.

PHOTO K: To ease alignment when applying larger pieces of plastic laminate, wait until the contact cement has tacked up and then lay dowels across the panels with the laminate on top centered over the panel. Press the laminate into the glue, working from the center outward and removing the dowels as you go.

PHOTO L: Bevel the sharp laminate edges using a mill file pushed at an angle to the edge.

PHOTO M: When rabbeting with a dado head, protect your saw's rip fence by attaching an auxiliary fence that's cut out to accommodate the cutter.

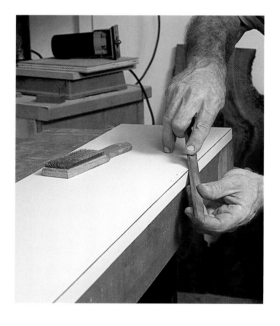

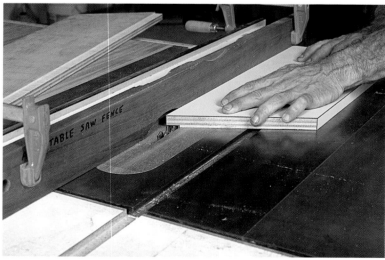

Assembling the Extension Tables

1. Glue the fronts and backs to the bases, with the unglued tops in place to help square the assembly (see photo P on p. 120).

2. After the glue cures, remove the top and plane a slight ramp on the last ½ in. or so of the exposed front and back sections of the left-hand table (see the drawing "Extension Table with Telescoping Arm" on p. 115). This will help the telescoping arm close easily.

3. Glue the tops in place, and immediately wipe away interior glue squeeze-out. Again, make sure everything is square under clamp pressure.

Making the Telescoping Arm

1. Mill the rails, ripping them to fit exactly between the top and base of the extension table.

2. Rout or saw the grooves for the stiffener panels (see the drawing "Extension Table with Telescoping Arm" on p. 115).

3. Cut the panels. To determine their exact width, clamp the rails inside the extension table and measure between the bottoms of the grooves.

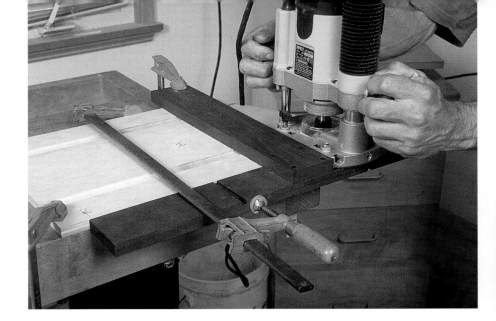

PHOTO N: To cut the lag-screw slots in the base, guide your router using a T-shaped jig clamped to the workpiece.

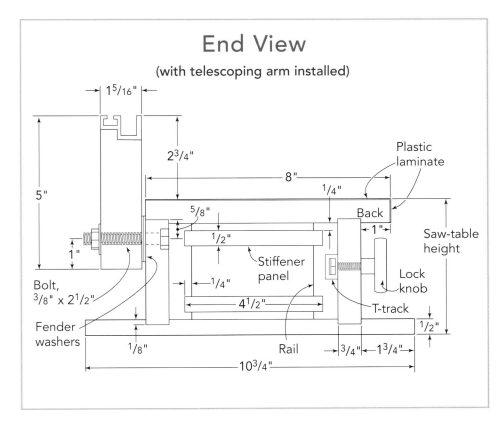

End View
(with telescoping arm installed)

1⁵/₁₆"
2³/₄"
5"
8"
¹/₄"
Plastic laminate
Back
5/8"
1/2"
Saw-table height
1"
1"
Stiffener panel
Lock knob
Bolt, ³/₈" x 2¹/₂"
1/4"
T-track
Fender washers
4¹/₂"
1/8"
Rail
3/4"
1³/₄"
1/2"
10³/₄"

PHOTO O: To cut the bolt-head recesses in the extension-table backs, insert a bolt into each hole and then trace around the head with a sharp pencil. Clean out the waste with a chisel, making the recess just slightly deeper than the head.

4. Working on a flat surface, glue the rails to the panels, keeping everything square.

5. After the glue cures, plane the faces of the rails for a snug but sliding fit inside the table. Wax the rails to reduce friction.

6. Saw or rout the T-track groove in the front rail, making sure it is exactly centered. Install the T-track.

Making the Fence

Although the aluminum half-track can be used on a ¾-in.-thick fence, I prefer a fence that's more substantial. I made mine from hard maple.

1. Make the left- and right-hand fences. I extended my right-hand fence to within ⅛ in. of the chopsaw fence. My left-hand fence sits 1 in. away from the saw fence, allowing finger access for adjusting small workpieces. Extend

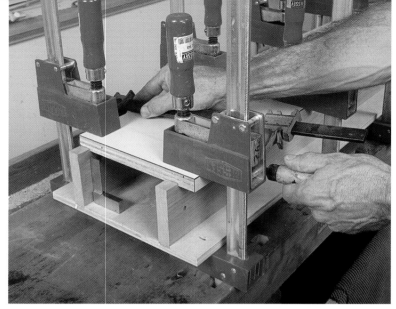

PHOTO P: When gluing each unit, draw the back tightly into its rabbet with a clamp. Immediately wipe up any interior glue squeeze-out with a damp rag on a stick (or have a skinny-armed helper do it).

the opposite end 2¼ in. past the end of the extension table.

2. Saw the ⅜-in. by ¼-in. rabbet in the top edge of each fence for the half-track.

3. Strike a line across the half-track 3¼ in. in from the left-hand end of the 36-in. piece. This will be your cutline for separating the arm section of the fence later. Mark out screw holes for attaching the track sections (see the drawing "Extension Table with Telescoping Arm" on p. 115). Drill and countersink the holes on the drill press.

4. Using the bolt holes in the extension tables as a reference, mark out the ⅜-in. by ¼-in. slots in the fences, centering them side to side over the bolt holes to allow lateral fence adjustment.

AND NOW FOR SOMETHING COMPLETELY DIFFERENT

Brian Boggs decided that he didn't need a full-length fence at all—just a sliding stop with a short section of fence attached to it to register the end of the workpiece. The sliding stop mounts onto two lengths of angle iron set at the saw-table height. An acrylic plate screwed into a mortise on the under-side of the stop block pro-vides a hairline cursor for use with the tape rule attached to the wooden strips that support the rails. The locking knob threads onto a bolt that passes through a mating block on the underside of the rails.

5. Rout the slots, centering them 1 in. up from the bottom of the fence as shown in the drawing "End View" on p. 119. Unless you have a long bit, you'll have to rout in from both sides.

6. Install the half-track on the fences (see photo Q).

7. Bolt the left-hand fence tightly to its extension table, with pairs of ⅟₁₆-in.-thick fender washers in between (see the drawing "Extension Table with Telescoping Arm" on p. 115). Position the fence the desired distance from the chopsaw fence, and mark a reference line across the fence and extension table for repositioning the fence later. Install the telescoping section, locking it tightly in place with its end protruding 2 in. from the extension table.

8. Make the spacer. It should be 1⅞ in. long and as wide as the rear rail. In thickness, it needs to fit exactly between the fence and the rear rail with the telescoping section tightly locked. Glue the spacer block to the rear rail, aligning the ends of both (see the drawing "Extension Table with Telescoping Arm" on p. 115).

9. Detach the fence, and use a carbide blade to cut off the 3-in.-long piece for the telescoping arm. Reinstall the main fence, aligning it with the reference marks you made earlier on the table. Also, install the fence on the right-hand table.

10. Lock the telescoping arm in place with 2 in. projecting from the extension table. (The ⅛-in. gap between the spacer and the end of the extension table will allow fence adjustment later.) Butt the arm section of the fence against the main fence, aligning them carefully, and glue the arm section to the spacer.

Installing the Tables

1. Using a long straightedge placed against the chopsaw fence and the table fences, position both extension tables on the cabinet top and mark their locations.

2. Remove the fences and arm, and mark the lag-screw locations in the centers of their slots. Drill pilot holes in the cabinet top, and bolt the tables loosely in place.

3. Apply a coat of finish to the fences, and reattach them, aligning the main fence with its reference mark on the table. Using a long straightedge, carefully align the extension-table fences with the chopsaw fence, and bolt the tables in place. Also, check that the tabletops are level with the saw table. If necessary, shim the bases to achieve this.

4. Attach the adhesive-backed tape rules to the half-track. I marked each fence 16 in. away from the blade and applied the tape, aligning its 16-in. increment with my line. Check your accuracy by making test cuts using flip stops aligned with the tape markings. If necessary, loosen the fence bolts and adjust the fence position.

5. Finish up by attaching the short top piece to the telescoping arm. To do this, install the arm, butting the sections of fence together. Glue the arm top to the rails, spacing it ⅟₁₆ in. away from the main top to allow for fine fence adjustments later, if necessary.

PHOTO Q: For accurate alignment when installing the half-track, attach a flip stop to the track and then clamp it against the face of the fence before drilling the track attachment screws.

Full house: The majority of the author's routers, bits, and accessories fit into his well-compartmentalized router cabinet.

ROUTER TABLE

I HAVE USED and tested a lot of shopmade and commercial router tables over the years, and I decided to design a router table that incorporated the best features of all of them. First and foremost, I wanted a top that would stay flat over time. The H-shaped understructure on this cabinet provides the necessary tabletop support, and the ¼-in.-thick aluminum insert plate stays flat even when suspending my heavy Porter Cable® 3¼-hp router. To prevent back strain and to increase router accessibility, I offset the router toward the front of the table. Much routing is done on narrow stock anyway, and when more support surface is needed, you can work from the end or back of the table. I omitted a miter-gauge track because I seldom need one and prefer to keep the tabletop free of recesses that trap chips.

Enclosing the router in the cabinet dampens noise and allows dust collection. Two electrical outlets wired to an easily accessible switch allow for switching on the router and shop vacuum at the same time.

For wheelbarrow-style mobility, two fixed casters are installed at one end of the cabinet, with the other end resting solidly on the floor for stability.

The trays that flank the router compartment hold bits, and the drawers in the lower section accommodate routers and accessories. I inset the trays and drawers to prevent chips from collecting on top of the fronts and then falling into the drawers. I avoided using commercial drawer slides to maximize interior space and to prevent drawers from opening when moving the cabinet.

I used a commercially made fence, but you can make your own. Dust collection at the fence can be handled several ways. You can connect its hose to the hose coming from the back of the cabinet using a Y-fitting, or you can run a jumper hose from the fence into the cabinet back. For heavy chip collection, you can hook a dust collector to the cabinet and hook the fence to a shop vacuum.

ROUTER TABLE

THE CASE JOINERY consists of dadoes and rabbets. The baffle reduces the size of the router compartment for better evacuation and provides central support against tabletop sag. The cutout at the bottom of the baffle provides an exit for chips, and the space under the central doors allows intake air to sweep the compartment. The power switch controls a receptacle box in the baffle (for the router plug) and a box in the back (for a shop vacuum), allowing simultaneous control of both tools.

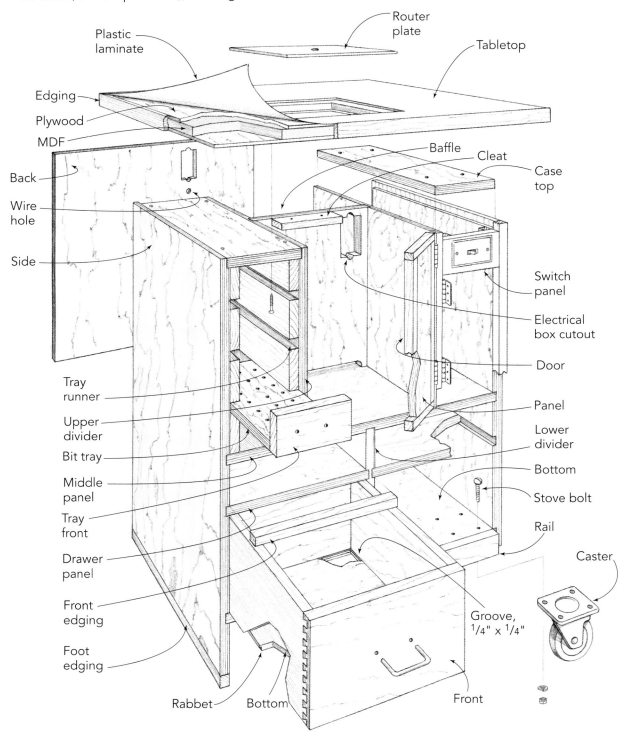

Elevations

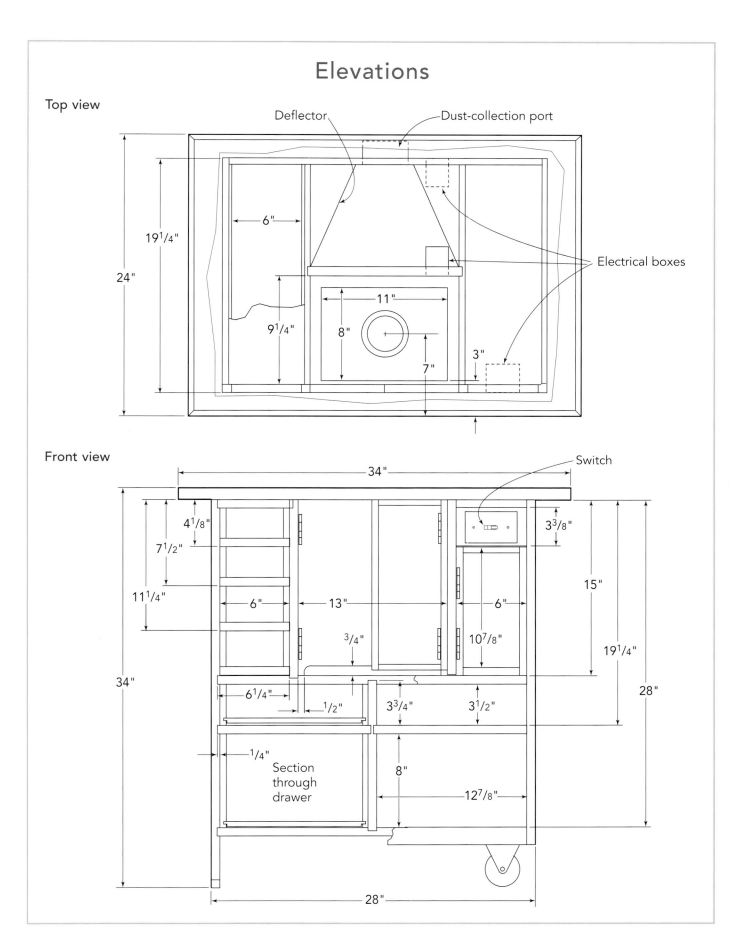

Top view

Deflector

Dust-collection port

Electrical boxes

19¹/₄"

24"

6"

9¹/₄"

11"

8"

7"

3"

Front view

Switch

34"

4¹/₈"

7¹/₂"

11¹/₄"

6"

13"

6"

3³/₈"

15"

19¹/₄"

28"

³/₄"

10⁷/₈"

34"

6¹/₄"

¹/₂"

3³/₄"

3¹/₂"

¹/₄"

Section through drawer

8"

12⁷/₈"

28"

CUT LIST FOR ROUTER TABLE

Top

1	Center panel	¾" x 23" x 33"	MDF
2	Outer panels	¼" x 23" x 33"	Hardboard or MDF
2	Edgings	½" x 1¼" x 24"	Solid wood
2	Edgings	½" x 1¼" x 34"	Solid wood

Case

1	Side	¾" x 19¼" x 29½"	Hardwood plywood
1	Side	¾" x 19¼" x 32¼"	Hardwood plywood
1	Lower divider	¾" x 18¾" x 12¾"	Hardwood plywood
2	Upper dividers	¾" x 18¾" x 15¼"	Hardwood plywood
2	Case tops	¾" x 18¾" x 6½"	Hardwood plywood
1	Middle panel	¾" x 18¾" x 27"	Hardwood plywood
2	Drawer panels	¾" x 18¾" x 13⅜"	Hardwood plywood
1	Bottom	¾" x 18¾" x 27"	Hardwood plywood
1	Baffle	¾" x 13½" x 15"	Hardwood plywood
1	Back	½" x 27" x 28¾"	Hardwood plywood
1	Front edging	¾" x ¾" x 29½"	Solid wood
1	Front edging	¾" x ¾" x 33"	Solid wood
2	Front edgings	¾" x ¾" x 15"	Solid wood
1	Front edging	¾" x ¾" x 12¼"	Solid wood
2	Front edgings	¾" x ¾" x 6"	Solid wood
1	Front edging	¾" x ¾" x 26½"	Solid wood
2	Front edgings	¾" x ¾" x 12⅞"	Solid wood
1	Rail	¾" x 1½" x 26½"	Solid wood
1	Foot edging	¾" x ¾" x 19¼"	Solid wood
1	Switch panel	¾" x 3⅜" x 6"	Solid wood
2	Switch-panel cleats	½" x ¾" x 3¼"	Solid wood
2	Deflectors	½" x 7⅝" x 27"	Cut both from one plywood panel.

Doors

1	Panel	¾" x 5" x 9⅞"	Hardwood plywood
2	Edgings	½" x ¾" x 5"	Solid wood
2	Edgings	½" x ¾" x 10⅞"	Solid wood
2	Panels	¾" x 5½" x 13⅝"	Hardwood plywood
4	Edgings	½" x ¾" x 5½"	Solid wood
4	Edgings	½" x ¾" x 14¼"	Solid wood

(continued on facing page)

The construction of the router table can be broken down into three basic processes: making the top; making the case; and making the doors, drawers, and trays. I built the top first, then the case. Finally, I made and fit the doors, drawers, and trays to fit their openings.

I made the top by sandwiching a piece of ¾-in.-thick MDF between two outer panels of ¼-in.-thick hardwood plywood. However, inconsistencies in the thickness of hardwood plywood prevent the top from being truly dead flat. If I had it to do again, I would use MDF or hardboard (such as Masonite®) for the outer panels, as I suggest in the cut list.

Making the Top

Laminating the panels

1. Saw the panels slightly oversize. You'll trim them to final length and width after gluing them together.

2. To prepare for glue-up, make crowned clamping cauls from thick lengths of hardwood about 24 in. long (see the drawing "Clamping Cauls" on p. 15).

3. Glue the panels together, working on a flat benchtop or table-saw top. I applied a thorough, even coat of yellow glue with a roller to one face of the center panel and one face of an outer panel. I clamped the assembly down to a 24-in.-wide benchtop with the outer panel underneath the center panel. After the glue cured, I attached the opposite panel in the same manner. If you don't have an appropriate-size benchtop, work on riser blocks and use a thick, flat panel as a caul to spread pressure over the outer panel.

Applying the edging and plastic laminate

1. Mill the ½-in.-thick solid-wood edging, making the pieces about 1⁄16 in. wider than the thickness of the top.

2. Dry-fit the edging to the top, carefully mitering the ends to meet neatly (see the left photo on p. 169). If you find that you've cut a miter too short, there's no harm in trimming the width or length of the top just a bit to make it fit.

PHOTO A: Using a router with a flush-trim subbase, cut the edging almost flush to the surfaces of the outer panels.

PHOTO B: Using a block plane set for a very fine cut, finish trimming the edging flush to the panels.

3. Glue the edging in place, applying plenty of glue to the porous edges of the MDF. I first glue both long pieces in place, using the dry-fit shorter pieces for alignment purposes. After the glue cures, I attach the shorter pieces.

4. Trim the edging flush to the panels. I first routed it just a hair proud of the panel (see photo A), then finished up with a few swipes of a finely set, sharp block plane (see photo B).

5. Cut the plastic laminate oversize, apply it to both sides of the top, and trim it flush to

CUT LIST FOR ROUTER TABLE (CONTINUED)

Trays			
4	Trays	¾" x 5 15⁄16" x 18½"	Hardwood plywood
2	Tray fronts	¾" x 3⅜" x 6"	Solid wood
2	Tray fronts	¾" x 3¾" x 6"	Solid wood
4	Tray runners	½" x 2 9⁄16" x 18¾"	Hardwood plywood
4	Tray runners	½" x 2 15⁄16" x 18¾"	Hardwood plywood
Drawers			
4	Sides	½" x 3½" x 18 5⁄16"	Solid wood
4	Fronts/backs	¾" x 3½" x 12 13⁄16"	Solid wood
4	Sides	½" x 8" x 18 5⁄16"	Solid wood
4	Fronts/backs	¾" x 8" x 12 13⁄16"	Solid wood
4	Bottoms	½" x 18¼" x 12 5⁄16"	Hardwood plywood
Hardware			
1	Aluminum router plate	¼" x 8" x 11"	From Rockler
6	Butt hinges	1¼" x 1½"	
2	Nonswiveling casters	3"	Woodcraft, item #141052
8	Flat-head stove bolts with washers and nuts	5⁄16" x 1¼"	
3	Adjustable ball catches		Woodcraft, item #27H39
11	Aluminum wire pulls	3"	Lee Valley, item #01W76.01
Electrical			
3	Metal receptacle boxes with surface-mount flanges	2" x 2½" x 3"	
1	Single-pole switch		
1	Switch plate		
2	Duplex receptacles		
2	Duplex receptacle plates		
1	SJ wire	12 12-ga.	
1	Plug		

A FLUSH-TRIM BASEPLATE

Here's a great router jig for trimming edging flush to panels. The jig simply consists of a sole plate and a heel plate as shown. In use, the jig suspends the router above the edging to be trimmed, with the bit extended down

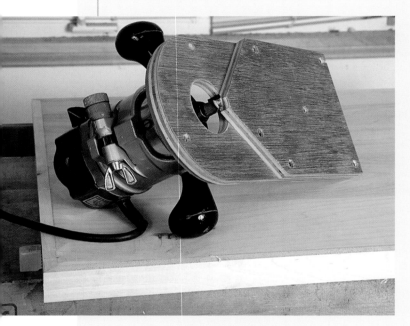

to the finished surface. The 45-degree cut-aways on the heel plate allow it access into corners.

To make the baseplate, cut the ½-in.-thick hardwood plywood blanks for the sole plate and heel plate, matching the width of the pieces to the diameter of your router base. Remove your router's subbase, and use it to transfer the locations of the router attachment screws onto the sole plate. Also, trace the perimeter of the subbase onto the sole plate to create your cut line. Drill and countersink the attachment holes, and drill the bit opening in the sole plate. (I chose to make a 2¼-in.-dia. opening for good visibility.)

Lay out and cut the heel to the shape shown. Drill screw holes for attaching it to the sole plate, countersinking the holes for flat-head screws or counterboring them for round-head screws. Also, drill a clearance hole through the sole plate to allow access to any screw in the sole plate that will be covered by the heel plate.

Screw the heel plate to the sole plate, and attach a mushroom-style handle. Finish up by sanding the plates and waxing the heel plate to minimize friction.

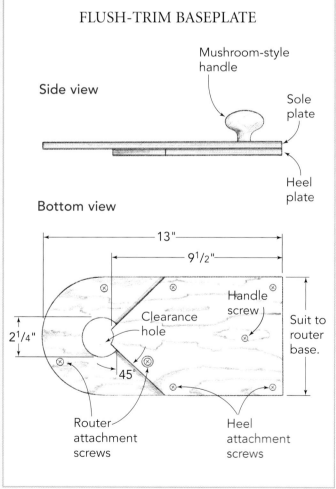

FLUSH-TRIM BASEPLATE

Side view

Mushroom-style handle

Sole plate

Heel plate

Bottom view

13"

9½"

2¼"

Clearance hole

Handle screw

45°

Suit to router base.

Router attachment screws

Heel attachment screws

the edging. (For more on applying plastic laminates, see "Laminating the Tops" on p. 115).

Installing the router plate

My router plate rests on a ½-in.-wide ledge recessed into the tabletop (see the drawing "Router Table" on p. 124). To mount the plate, I first drill out the radius for each corner of the recess using a Forstner bit, then I make the table cutout. Last, I rout the ledges.

1. Check your top with a straightedge. If it's crowned, orient the crown on the top side. Locate the plate, as shown in the drawing "Elevations" on p. 125, and trace around its edges with a fine pencil line. Mark for the table-cutout lines ½ in. in from the plate outline.

2. Prepare to drill the corners of the cutout by drilling a guide hole in a panel that you'll clamp to the top to prevent the bit from skittering on the plastic laminate. Drill the 1-in.-dia. hole on the drill press.

3. Now make a hole-depth gauge. Cut two disks that are slightly less than 1 in. in diameter. Make one disk the exact thickness of the router plate and the other disk the thickness of your guide-hole panel. Cut one disk into a mushroom shape as shown in photo C. (The stem of the mushroom simply provides a handle.) Glue the two disks together.

4. Clamp the guide-hole panel to the top, with its hole aligned with the plate corner lines. Drill to a depth that equals the thickness of the depth gauge. It's all right if you drill a bit too deep because the plate will be resting primarily on the straight sections of the ledges.

5. Saw or rout the through cutout in the top, following your layout lines. You don't have to be precise with these cuts.

PHOTO D: Rout the ledges around the table cutout using a straightedge to guide your router. Here, the scrap from the cutout supports the straightedge, which overhangs the top when cutting the foremost ledge.

6. Rout the ledges using a straight-edged board as a guide (see photo D). Try to get the plate dead-flush to the surface or just a hair proud of it. But don't worry if you rout a bit too deep; you can shim with tape later.

7. After testing the fit of the plate, screw it to your router base (after removing the router's subbase). If necessary, notch the cutout ledges to accommodate your router handles or other protrusions.

TIP

To keep the contact cement on your brush or roller from drying out between applications, wrap the tool tightly in plastic between uses.

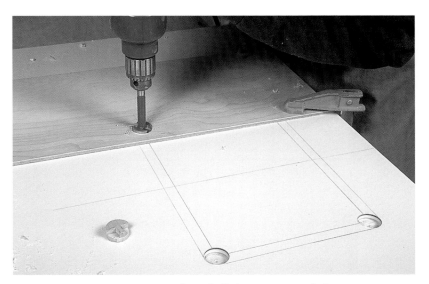

PHOTO C: Using a Forstner bit, drill the corners of the cutout to a depth that matches the thickness of the router plate. A panel with a guide hole prevents the bit from wandering. The thickness of the depth gauge in the foreground equals the combined thickness of the router plate plus the thickness of the guide-hole panel.

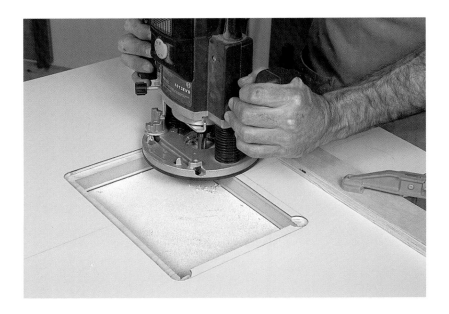

A BENCHTOP ROUTER TABLE

If you don't have the space for a full-size router-table cabinet, a benchtop model may be just the ticket. Andy Rae's benchtop table is a good example of an easily made design, which includes the basic features you'll probably want. A top panel mounts to a simple box, with the router base screwed directly to the underside of the top. An auxiliary switch provides accessible power control. A plywood fence that includes a dust-collection port attaches via slots to knobs that screw into threaded inserts in the tabletop, and a miter-gauge slot cut into the top guides a shop-made miter gauge when needed.

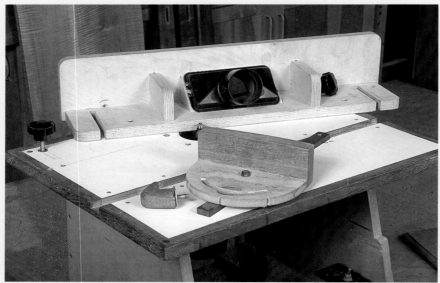

Making the Case

Making the case involves cutting, fitting, and edging the plywood panels, then mortising for hinges, attaching the tray runners, and making the cutouts for the electrical boxes all before assembling the case pieces. This is necessary because the relatively small compartments make cutting-tool access difficult after case assembly.

Cutting the pieces

1. Lay out the plywood pieces for the case.
2. Cut the plywood pieces to size. Leave the back ¼ in. or so oversize in width for now. You'll trim it for an exact fit after assembling the case.
3. Mill the pieces for the edging to ¾ in. thick, but make them slightly oversize in width for now, as you'll trim them flush to the plywood after attaching them. The sizes

PHOTO E: When sawing dadoes with a dado head on the table saw, keep the workpiece solidly against the rip fence and maintain constant downward pressure near the joint.

in the cut list give the finished lengths; however, you should make the pieces about ⅜ in. longer than their finished length for now. You'll trim them to fit later.

Cutting the joints

1. Arrange the pieces for placement, and mark them. I use the triangle marking system (see the drawing on p. 14).

2. Lay out the dadoes and rabbets (see the drawing "Elevations" on p. 125). Make sure to carefully center the dadoes in the middle panel and bottom.

3. Saw or rout the dadoes (see photo E).

4. Saw the rabbets at the tops of the sides and upper dividers using an auxiliary fence on your table-saw rip fence (see photo F).

5. Saw ½-in.-wide rabbets in the rear edges of the sides to accept the back. Stop the rabbets at the bottom dadoes.

Applying and trimming the edging

1. Glue the foot edging to the taller case side to prevent tearout of the plywood side at the bottom when moving the cabinet. After the glue dries, trim the edging's ends flush to the edges of the plywood.

2. Glue and clamp the edging to the rest of the pieces (see photo G on p. 132). Make sure that the edging overhangs both faces of the panel. On pieces where the ends of the edging will abut other edging—such as on all

of the horizontal pieces—make sure that the edging is set back no more than ³⁄₁₆ in. from the end of the panel.

3. Trim all of the edging flush to the panels in the same manner that you trimmed the edging for the top.

4. Saw the ends of the edging on the cabinet sides flush to the ends of the panels (see photo H on p. 132). Do the same at the top edges of the upper dividers.

5. Trim away the ends of any edging where a panel will tuck into a joint (see photo I on p. 132).

PHOTO F: Sawing rabbets on the table saw requires the use of an auxiliary fence to prevent cutting into your saw's rip fence.

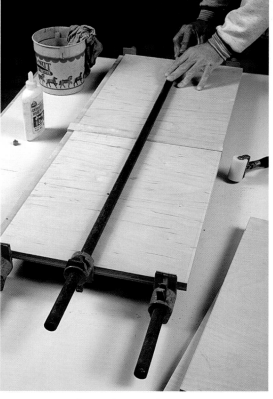

PHOTO G: When gluing edging on similarly
sized panels, sandwich the edging between
the two panels. Alternate clamps over and
under to prevent the workpieces from buckling under pressure.

PHOTO H: To saw edging flush to
the ends of panels, align a shim block
flush with the outside face of the
sawblade teeth.

PHOTO I: To cut the notch where the end of a panel slips into
a joint, the author uses a good dado head and an auxiliary rip
fence. A miter gauge guides the workpiece, with a piece of
scrap backing up the cut to minimize exit tearout.

Cutting out the baffle, cutting the hinge mortises, and drilling for the casters

There are a few cuts you need to make before
assembling the case, as it will be difficult to
maneuver tools within the compartments
after assembly.

1. Lay out and cut the ¾-in.-wide by
12-in.-long scalloped cutout at the bottom
of the baffle (see the drawing "Elevations"
on p. 125).

2. Lay out and cut the opening for the electrical box in the upper right-hand section of
the baffle (see photo J on facing page). The
placement isn't critical; just leave enough
room at the edges to accommodate the cover
plate. Also, drill a hole for the wire that passes
through the upper rear section of the right-
hand upper divider (see photo R on p. 136).

3. Lay out the hinge mortises in the upper
dividers, locating them ¾ in. from where
the doors end. (Don't forget to factor in the

APPLYING SOLID-WOOD EDGING

The primary purpose of solid-wood edging is to hide the unsightly edges of plywood. However, a secondary purpose can be to cover rabbets, dadoes, and other case joints. You have several options for applying edging, and it can be done either before or after the case is assembled.

The easiest approach is to edge the panels before cutting your joints. This means that you'll be cutting the joints right through the edging, exposing the rabbets and dadoes, as seen in the drawing "Assembly Table" on p. 162. The advantage is that the oversize edging can be glued on, then easily trimmed flush to the pieces before assembly.

A second option is to fit and apply the edging after the plywood pieces have been assembled. This covers the joints, but makes trimming the edging a bit more difficult, especially in corners. In these circumstances, I first use a flush-trim router bit, then pare the overhang near the corners with a chisel where the router bit won't reach. I finish up by scraping and sanding.

Another approach, which was used for this router table, is to apply the edging to the panels after cutting the joints. Before assembly, the ends of the edging are trimmed where the panels fit into the joints. This covers the joints but allows trimming the edging flush to the plywood before assembly. This is often the best approach when dealing with many compartments.

⅜-in. opening below the center doors.) Trace around the hinges using a sharp knife (see photo K on p.134).

4. Cut the mortises. I first rout them as close to my knife lines as is safely possible (see photo L on p. 134). Then I pare to the knife lines using a sharp chisel (see photo M on p. 134).

5. Drill the pilot holes for the screws, offsetting them slightly to pull the hinges toward the rear of the mortises.

6. Drill and countersink for the flat-head caster stove bolts. To locate the holes, set each caster plate in ½ in. from the end of the bottom panel and ¼ in. in from the front or rear edge.

PHOTO J: Use a drill press and jigsaw to cut out the electrical-box opening in the baffle.

TIP

To prevent snapping the heads of small brass screws, prethread the pilot hole by first installing a steel screw of the same size.

PHOTO K: Lay out each door hinge by tracing around the leaf with a sharp knife. Take light initial passes to avoid shoving the hinge, then deepen the cuts using a square and marking gauge.

Dry-fitting and predrilling the case

Before gluing up the case, I dry-fit the parts and predrill for the screws. This makes the glue-up go faster and prevents fouling my bit with glue.

1. The first step in assembling the case is to either glue and nail or staple the tray runners to the left-hand side and upper divider (see the drawing "Elevations "on p. 125). To prevent glue squeeze-out, don't spread glue near the edges. Before attaching the runners, I sanded their edges to 220 grit and applied wax for easy tray sliding.

2. Using a large square, mark the screw paths on the panels opposite the joints to be attached with screws.

3. Dry-fit the baffle and upper dividers to the middle panel and then drill and countersink screw holes for attaching them. Make sure that the top edges of all the pieces are carefully aligned.

4. Dry-fit the entire case, except for the shelves. Stand the unit upside down. Drill and countersink for attaching the bottom to the lower divider and for attaching the middle panel to the upper dividers. Avoid the baffle dadoes when drilling the middle panel.

5. Stand the unit right side up. Drill for four screws through the middle panel into the lower divider.

6. While the unit is dry-assembled, cut the back to fit snugly between its rabbets. You'll use the back to help keep the case square while the glue cures after assembly.

7. The last thing to do in preparation for glue-up is to make six clamping cauls, about 19 in. long, from thick hardwood. You'll need them for clamping the sides in place. Plane a

PHOTO L: Rout as close to your knife lines as is safely possible.

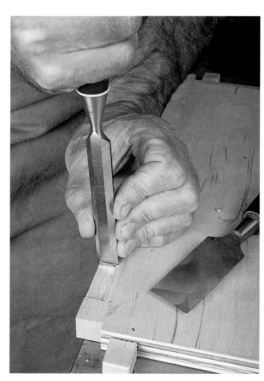

PHOTO M: Finish up by using sharp chisels to pare to your knife lines.

$\frac{1}{16}$-in. crown on one edge of each caul to distribute pressure at the center of the panel. Alternatively, you could nail or screw the sides in place, puttying or plugging the holes later.

Gluing up the case

Now you're ready to glue everything together. You'll want to work quickly, so make sure that your screws, clamps, cauls, and wiping rag are at the ready.

1. Using #6 by 2-in. screws, glue and screw the middle panel to one of the upper dividers. Then glue and screw one end of the baffle to that divider. Last, glue and screw the opposite divider to the baffle, and attach the middle panel to that baffle. Make sure the top edges of the baffle are carefully aligned with the top edges of the dividers.

2. With the case facedown on the assembly table, glue the shelves to the lower divider, then glue the sides to the bottom, shelves, and middle panel. With the back dry-fit in place, I clamped one end of a caul to each joint and then stood the case upside down to clamp the opposite ends of the cauls (see photos N and O).

3. Glue and clamp the two tops into their rabbets, and glue a screw cleat to the top of the baffle for attaching the top later.

4. Attach the casters using the stove bolts, washers, and nuts. I included lock washers because of the vibration inherent in a router table.

5. Plane or sand the front edges of the case flush to each other.

Making the deflectors

The two triangular deflectors in the rear cavity were suggested by a dust-collection expert as a means of targeting airflow toward the dust-collection port in the cabinet back. Good advice? All I know is that the dust collection in this router table works well.

1. Make a cardboard pattern of the deflector shape as shown in the drawing "Deflector" on p. 136.

2. Saw a piece of ½-in.-thick hardwood plywood to 7⅝ in. by 27 in.

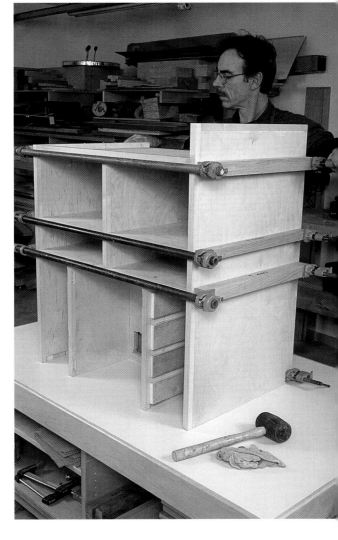

PHOTOS N AND O: With the back dry-fit in place and the unit facedown, clamp one end of each caul to the case (above). Stand the case upside down, clamp the other ends, and carefully adjust each clamp so it's centered across its joint (right).

Deflector

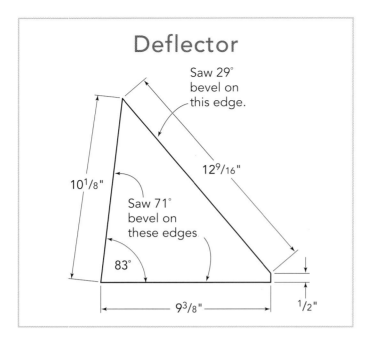

Saw 29° bevel on this edge.

12⁹/₁₆"

10¹/₈"

Saw 71° bevel on these edges

83°

9³/₈"

1/2"

3. Screw the plywood to a thick, squared-up piece of scrap at least 27 in. long. Set your sawblade at a 29-degree angle, and rip the bevel on one edge of the panel (see photo P).

4. Lay out a left-hand and right-hand deflector in mirrored fashion on the panel, aligning the long leg of each triangle along the beveled edge. Separate the two triangles with a square crosscut across the panel.

5. Set your sawblade to a 19-degree angle, and tack each triangle to a single-runner sled to cut the bevels on the 10⅛-in. edge and the 9⅜-in. edge (see photo Q). Save the offcuts.

6. Nip off the tip of each deflector where it fits against the baffle. I did this on the band-saw, with the table set at 19 degrees. Note

PHOTO P: The first step in making the twin deflectors is to saw the 29-degree bevel on the panel you'll use for both pieces. To make the cut safely, screw the panel to a piece of squared-up scrap lumber. (The groove in the scrap here is irrelevant.)

PHOTO Q: To make the 71-degree bevels on the deflectors, tack them solidly to a single-runner sled and make the cuts with the blade set at a 19-degree angle.

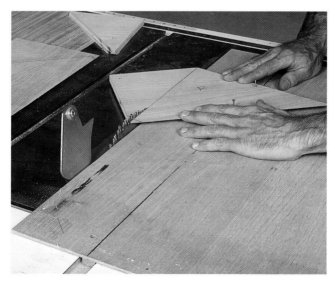

PHOTO R: When installing the deflectors, shape the offcuts to serve as backup blocks. (Note: The hole in the upper section of the divider is for the switch wire.)

that this bevel opposes the direction of the others.

7. With a bandsaw or jigsaw, shape the off-cuts you saved to serve as backup blocks for installing the deflectors. The bevel on each offcut is a perfect complementary angle to the standing angle of the deflectors (see photo R on the facing page). Glue and nail or staple the deflectors in place.

Preparing and installing the back

1. Make the cutout for the electrical box in the back and drill a hole for the incoming wire. I located the cutout 2 in. down from the top and 1 in. in from the right-hand upper divider. I drilled the hole for the wire 4 in. down from the cutout.

2. Drill or cut out the opening for your dust-collection port, locating it at the bottom center of the rear cabinet chamber, as close to the middle panel as your fitting allows. The type of opening and attachment will depend on whatever particular fitting you need to suit your shop vacuum or dust collector.

3. If you decide to use a jumper hose from your fence into the cabinet back, cut that opening now.

4. Glue and nail the back into its rabbets.

Installing the switch panel

1. Mill a piece of ¾-in.-thick by 3⅜-in.-wide stock 12 in. long to use for the switch panel. The extra length allows you to clamp the workpiece to the bench for making the electrical-box cutout.

2. Lay out and cut the opening for the electrical box, and crosscut the panel to fit exactly between the upper divider and side.

3. Make the switch-panel cleats. Glue them to the upper divider and side, carefully setting them back the exact thickness of the switch panel.

4. After the glue cures on the cleats, glue and clamp the panel to the cleats and the cabinet top.

A HORIZONTAL ROUTER-TABLE JIG

When routing the edges of wide boards or panels, it can be advantageous to lay the workpiece on the table and feed it against a horizontally mounted router. Mike Callihan added a pivoting panel to the edge of his router tabletop that allows him that capability. The panel pivots on a bolt at one end, while the other end is adjusted to the proper height, then secured by a bolt running through an arced slot. A substantial rail attached to the underside of the table serves as a backup for the jig to ensure that it's square to the tabletop.

Making the Trays, Drawers, and Doors

Now that the case is complete, it's time to make the trays, drawers, and doors and fit them to their openings.

Making the bit trays

1. Cut the plywood trays to size, and lay out the holes to hold your bits. I drilled an array of holes to hold my current collection of bits as well as future acquisitions. I drilled the holes ½ in. deep on the drill press, using drill bits slightly larger in diameter than my router-bit shanks.

2. Make the tray fronts, and attach them to the trays as shown in the drawing "Router Table" on p. 124. I used a couple of #20 biscuits to align and reinforce the joint, but if you don't have a biscuit joiner, it's all right to just edge-glue them to the trays. Make sure that the pieces align at the bottom and that the fronts are square to the trays under clamp pressure.

3. Fit the trays on their runners, and plane the edges for a small consistent gap all around each tray front.

Making the drawers

Although I built my drawers using dovetail joints for maximum strength, you could use any number of other joints, including routed drawer lock joints (see the sidebar "Routed Drawer Lock Joint" on pp. 154–55).

1. Mill the stock for the drawers. I ripped it to a width that exactly matched the height of the drawer openings because I plane the drawers for a close fit after assembly. Cross-cut the pieces to length, adjusting the length of the sides as necessary to suit any alternative joint you're using.

2. Mark all of the parts for orientation. I used the triangle marking system (see the drawing on p. 14).

3. Cut the joints. I used a dovetail jig to cut ½-in. half-blind dovetails at the front and back of the drawers (see photo S).

PHOTO S: Use a half-blind dovetail jig to quickly rout the drawer joints.

HALF-BLIND DOVETAIL JIGS

I enjoy cutting dovetails by hand, especially for fine furniture. But when it comes to quickly cranking out lots of utility-grade drawers, it's hard to beat the efficiency of a dovetail jig. There are a lot of dovetail jigs on the market, some of which will cut half-blind and through dovetails, as well as variably spaced tails. These premium jigs are versatile but expensive. However, if you just want a jig for making drawer joints, you can pick up a half-blind dovetail jig for less than a hundred dollars.

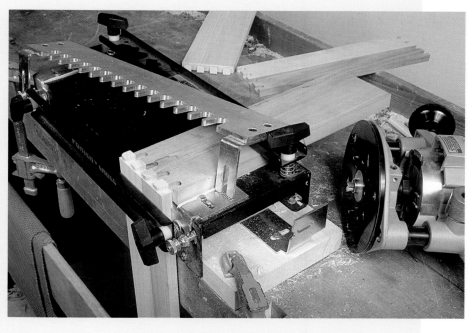

The design of these jigs is really ingenious. The pin board and tail board are mounted at right angles in the jig so that the tails and pins are cut at the same time. End stops offset the pieces so they'll line up properly during assembly. A template guide mounted on the router follows the fingers of a template to steer the bit.

You'll probably find the initial setup of one of these jigs to be a bit finicky, but once things are adjusted properly, you can cut joint after joint like a breeze. That said, be aware that because the spacing of the tails is fixed by the template, you may have to design the height of your drawers to suit the template spacing if you want your joints to terminate with a half pin at each end, which mimics a traditionally made joint.

4. Saw or rout the ¼-in. by ¼-in. drawer-bottom groove in all the parts. Run the groove through the tails, not the pins, so it won't be exposed on the sides of the drawers (see the drawing "Router Table" on p. 124).

5. Cut the drawer bottoms to size. Saw or rout a ¼-in. by ⁵⁄₁₆-in. rabbet on every edge to create the tongue that slips into the grooves.

6. Dry-assemble the drawers to make sure all the parts fit well.

7. Glue up the drawers (see photo T on p. 140). I use white glue for this because it has a longer open-assembly time than yellow glue. Spread a thorough coat on the tails and pins. I just spot-glue the bottoms at the center of every groove. If your joints fit well, you shouldn't need to clamp the drawers, but make sure they're square. Let the glue dry thoroughly.

PHOTO T: Because of its longer open-assembly time, white glue is better than yellow glue when assembling dove-tailed drawers.

Installing the drawers

1. Plane the bottom of each drawer so that it sits absolutely flat.

2. Fit each drawer into its opening, planing the sides and top edges as necessary for an easy-sliding fit. Aim for a consistent, small gap all around the sides. To create the gap at the bottom of each front, I planed a slight upward bevel on it.

3. Make the drawer stops—which are simply small blocks of wood that fit between the back of the drawer and the cabinet back—positioning the drawer front flush to the front of the cabinet. My pieces were about ⁷⁄₁₆ in. square by 4 in. long. Dab a bit of glue on the blocks, and simply rub them into place. Do *not* insert the drawer while the glue is curing, or seepage may glue the drawer in place. (I really should have known better . . .)

TIP

When ripping plywood into pieces, plan your cut sequence so that all factory edges are cut away in the process, leaving clean-cut edges.

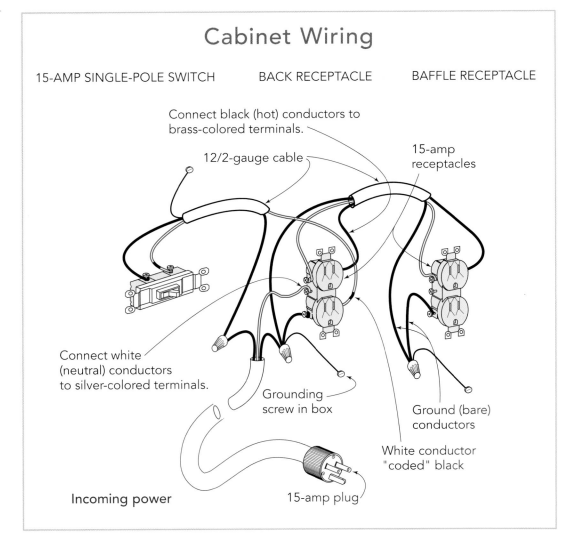

Cabinet Wiring

15-AMP SINGLE-POLE SWITCH   BACK RECEPTACLE   BAFFLE RECEPTACLE

Connect black (hot) conductors to brass-colored terminals.

12/2-gauge cable

15-amp receptacles

Connect white (neutral) conductors to silver-colored terminals.

Grounding screw in box

Ground (bare) conductors

White conductor "coded" black

Incoming power

15-amp plug

ROUTER-TABLE FENCES

Of course, you'll need a fence for your new router table. There is no shortage of commercial models (see Sources on p. 172), which are regularly reviewed in woodworking magazines. There are also plenty of shopmade designs published in woodworking books and magazines.

At its simplest, a fence needs to be only a span of thick, straight wood that clamps to the edges of the tabletop, with a cutout at the center to accommodate the bit. The next step up—which provides a higher fence—is to glue together a couple of straight, flat boards in the shape of an L. The bottom board is clamped to the router tabletop, and the vertical board includes a cutout for the router bit. Better designs include a dust-collection port and a means for adjustable attachment to the tabletop, as seen on the benchtop router table in the sidebar on p. 130. The best fence designs incorporate a two-piece split fence, which can be adjusted so that the two pieces closely flank the router bit to create a zero-clearance opening.

Making and installing the doors and applying a finish

1. Build the doors by applying solid-wood edging to the panels (which you probably do pretty well by now).

2. Screw the hinges into their mortises in the case. Press the edge of each door against the hinges, and use a sharp knife to transfer the locations of the leaf edges onto the doors (see the photo on p. 53). Cut the mortises in the doors as you did for the case mortises.

3. Screw the doors to the hinges with one screw per hinge, and mark the edges of the doors for a small, consistent gap all around. Remove the doors, and plane to your marks using a sharp plane. Also, plane a slight back bevel on the edges opposite the hinges.

4. At this point, I removed the hinges and applied several coats of wiping varnish to the doors, drawers, and tray fronts, as well as all exposed surfaces on the cabinet.

Installing the hardware and electrical components

1. Drill the holes for the drawer, tray, and door pulls and install them. I located the door pulls ¾ in. in from the edges of the doors, with the side door pull at the same height as the center pulls.

2. Install the hinges and catches. For the center doors, I used brass ball catches, which adjust for tension but require painfully precise alignment during installation. Use any catches you like.

3. Install the electrical components as shown in the drawing "Cabinet Wiring" on the facing page. The wiring isn't difficult to do, but if you don't feel comfortable with it, enlist the help of someone who does.

Attaching the top and selecting a fence

1. Align the top on the case with an even overhang all around, and clamp the top in place.

2. To ensure a tight connection, drill pilot holes into the tabletop and drill clearance holes through the case tops and plastic laminate. For strength when rolling the cabinet around, I used six #6 by 1⅝-in. drywall screws through each case top. Also, install one or two screws through the baffle cleat to pull down any crown in the top.

3. Buy or make a fence for your table.

One of the best helpers you can enlist in your shop is a multi-drawer, mobile cabinet for rolling your collection of tools to wherever they're needed.

MOBILE TOOL CABINET

YOUR SHOP doesn't have to be neat as a pin to be organized and efficient, but a shop that's cluttered by homeless tools and supplies isn't going to make your workday easier, as you pick through piles of stuff to find that blasted #3 Phillips driver. Organization can also save you money. I'm sure I'm not the only person who has occasionally dropped a few dollars buying a duplicate wrench or set of hinges simply because I misplaced the ones I knew I had somewhere!

There are plenty of options for storing tools and supplies—ranging from racks, shelves, boxes, and bins to cabinets with drawers and customized compartments. Standard kitchen-style cabinets will accommodate many tools and supplies, but custom storage projects designed to suit specific contents can really pay off in organization. Not only will they allow you to quickly lay your hands on specific tools

and supplies, but they also permit a quick inventory of the contents.

Bill Hylton's tool cabinet is a great example of efficient organization. And like any well-crafted toolbox, it represents the skills of the craftsman who uses it. The cabinet's legs and rails are made of solid ash. For the panels, Hylton used ash-veneered MDF, which he biscuit-joined to the case framework. The top is a piece of secondhand butcher-block countertop. Full-extension drawer slides allow easy access to every tool in a drawer, and some of the drawers have flocked, French-fit inserts with custom recesses cut out for dedicated storage of specific tools. Hylton's shop-made pulls are scaled to the sizes of the drawers and increase in size from top to bottom for a nice design flair. Heavy-duty casters allow easy moving of the cabinet to wherever it's needed during the workday.

MOBILE TOOL CABINET

ALL OF THE RAILS, except the top front rail, join to the legs with loose tenons; the top front rail joins with dovetails. The back, bottom, and side panels connect to the rails and legs with #20 biscuits. The drawer boxes are constructed with drawer lock joints at the corners and are mounted to the case with commercial drawer slides. Solid-wood drawer fronts are screwed to the boxes afterward.

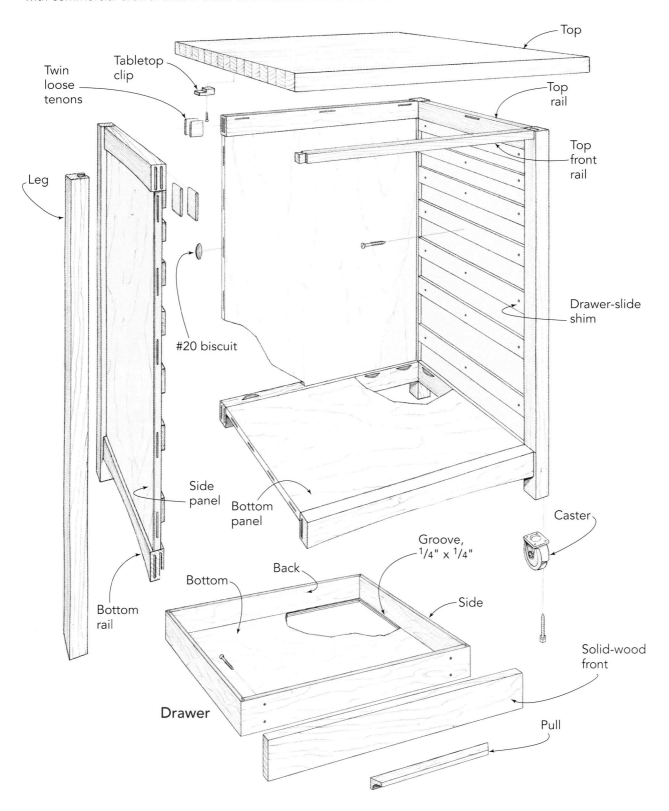

Elevations

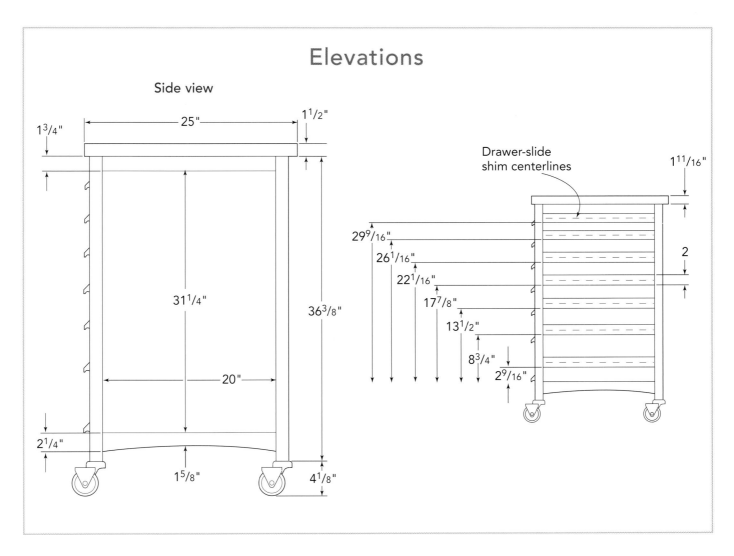

Side view

25"   1¹/₂"

1³/₄"

1³/₄"

31¹/₄"

36³/₈"

20"

2¹/₄"

1⁵/₈"

4¹/₈"

Drawer-slide shim centerlines

1¹¹/₁₆"

29⁹/₁₆"

26¹/₁₆"

22¹/₁₆"

17⁷/₈"

13¹/₂"

8³/₄"

2⁹/₁₆"

2

As when making any case of drawers, it's best to make the case first, then build the drawers to fit.

Building the Case

Milling the solid-wood parts

1. Mill the legs and rails to the sizes in the cut list. It's important that all the pieces be straight, flat, and square (see the sidebar "Dressing Stock with Machines" on p. 13). Make at least one of the legs about an inch oversize in length. After ripping and planing it, crosscut it to length and save the offcut to make a drilling jig for boring the caster bolt holes later.

2. If you're going to make your own top, instead of using manufactured butcher block

like Hylton did, glue up the boards to make the top. After the glue dries, sand or plane the top and then cut it to size.

Mortising the legs and rails

1. Lay out the mortises for joining the rails to the legs with loose tenons (see the drawing "Joints" on p. 148). If you use a mortising jig like Hylton's, you only need to lay out one pair of tenons to full width and length. The rest need only a centerline along the length of the mortises (see the sidebar "A Mortising Jig" on p. 149).

2. Set up the mortising jig to rout the mortises in the ends of the rails. Clamp one of the bottom rails to the jig, with its inner face clamped against the jig and its end aligned with the top of the jig. Align the mortise centerline with the registration line on the

Elevations (continued)

Front view

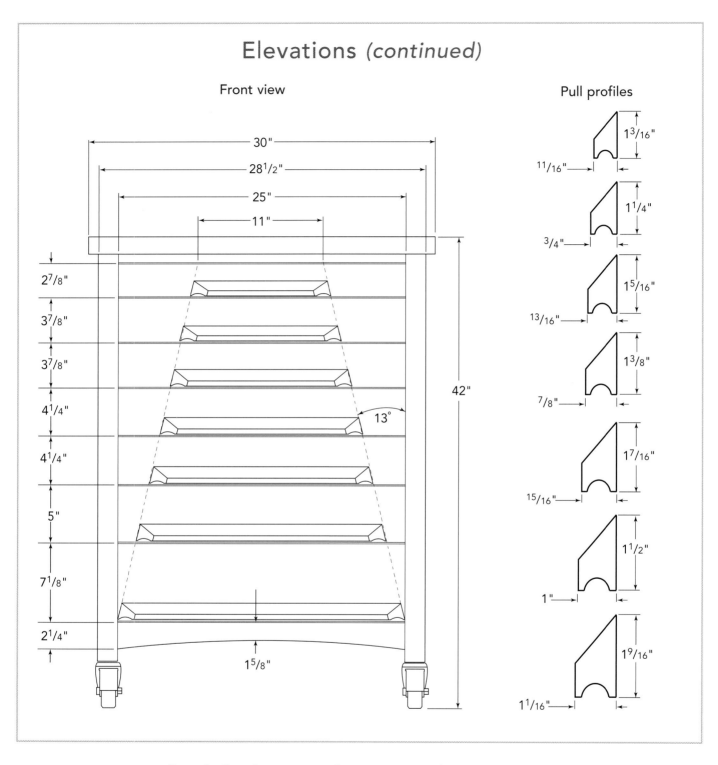

Pull profiles

jig, and adjust the router-travel stops to cut a 1⅝-in.-long mortise. Set your plunge router for a 1-in.-deep cut. Place a ⅜-in.-thick spacer against the rear of the jig, and adjust your router's edge guide to rout the innermost mortise (see photo A on facing page).

3. Rout the innermost mortise. Afterward, reposition the spacer behind the edge-guide

fence to shift the router forward for cutting the outermost mortise (see photo B on facing page).

4. Rout all of the bottom rail mortises in the same manner.

5. Rout the top rail mortises, which are ⅜ in. shorter than the bottom rail mortises. To account for the difference, place a ¾₆-in.-thick

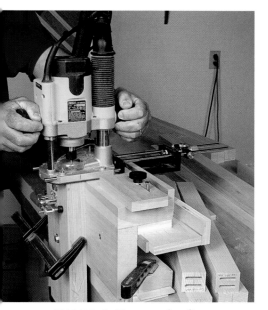

PHOTO A: To rout the first mortises in the end of a rail, mount the rail to the mortising jig, clamping it to the vertical work holder. Make the cut with a ⅝-in.-thick spacer placed between the edge-guide fenceand the rear of the jig.

PHOTO B: To rout the second rail mortise, reposition the ⅝-in.-thick spacer behind the edge-guide fence, which shifts the router forward.

CUT LIST FOR MOBILE TOOL CABINET

Top

1	Butcher-block top	1½" x 25" x 30"	Maple

Case

4	Posts	1¾" x 1¾" x 36⅜"	Hardwood
2	Bottom side rails	1⅝" x 2¼" x 20"	Hardwood
2	Top side rails	1⅝" x 1¾" x 20"	Hardwood
2	Bottom front/back rails	1⅝" x 2¼" x 25"	Hardwood
1	Top back rail	1⅝" x 1¾" x 25"	Hardwood
1	Top front rail	¾" x 1⅝" x 26½"	Hardwood
2	Sides	¾" x 20" x 31¼"	Veneered MDF
1	Back	¾" x 25" x 31¼"	Veneered MDF
1	Bottom	¾" x 20" x 25"	Birch plywood

Drawers

1	Applied front	¾" x 2⅞" x 25"	Hardwood
2	Fronts/backs	½" x 2⅝" x 24"	Baltic birch plywood
2	Sides	½" x 2⅝" x 19⅞"	Baltic birch plywood
2	Applied fronts	¾" x 3⅞" x 25"	Hardwood
4	Fronts/backs	½" x 3⅝" x 24"	Baltic birch plywood
4	Sides	½" x 3⅝" x 19⅞"	Baltic birch plywood
2	Applied fronts	¾" x 4¼" x 25"	Hardwood
4	Fronts/backs	½" x 4" x 24"	Baltic birch plywood
4	Sides	½" x 4" x 19⅞"	Baltic birch plywood
1	Applied front	¾" x 5" x 25"	Hardwood
2	Fronts/backs	½" x 4¾" x 24"	Baltic birch plywood
2	Sides	½" x 4¾" x 19⅞"	Baltic birch plywood
1	Applied front	¾" x 7⅛" x 25"	Hardwood
2	Fronts/backs	½" x 6⅞" x 24"	Baltic birch plywood
2	Sides	½" x 6⅞" x 19⅞"	Baltic birch plywood
7	Bottoms	¼" x 23⁷⁄₁₆" x 19⁷⁄₁₆"	Birch plywood
2	Drawer-slide shims	½" x 1¹¹⁄₁₆" x 20"	MDF or plywood
12	Drawer-slide shims	½" x 2" x 20"	MDF or plywood
7	Pulls	See the drawing "Elevations" on facing page.	

Hardware

7 sets Drawer slides Accuride® series 3832		20", full extension	Rockler, part #32508
4	Locking swivel casters	3"	Woodcraft, item #140639
4	Hex-head bolts	½"-13 x 1½"	

Joints

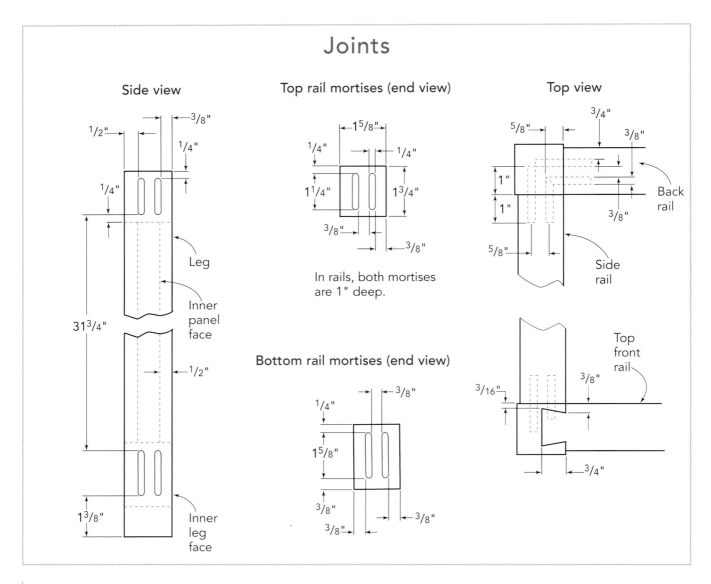

Side view

3/8"

1/2"

1/4"

1/4"

1/4"

Leg

31³/4"

Inner panel face

1/2"

1³/8"

Inner leg face

Top rail mortises (end view)

1⁵/8"

1/4"

1/4"

1¹/4"

1³/4"

3/8"

3/8"

In rails, both mortises are 1" deep.

Bottom rail mortises (end view)

3/8"

1/4"

1⁵/8"

3/8"

3/8"

3/8"

Top view

3/4"

5/8"

3/8"

1"

1"

Back rail

5/8"

Side rail

Top front rail

3/16"

3/8"

3/4"

shim against the end of each router-travel stop. After aligning the mortise centerline with the jig's registration line, rout the mortises in the same manner as before.

6. Rout the mortises in the legs. Clamp a leg to the jig, with one inner face against the face of the jig and the other inner face aligned with the top of the jig. Align the mortise centerline with the jig's registration line as before. Set one of your plunge router's turret stops for a ⅝-in.-deep cut and another for a 1-in.-deep cut. Leave the router-travel stops set up as they were.

7. Cut the outermost mortise to a depth of 1 in. Insert your ⅝-in.-thick spacer between the rear edge of the jig and the edge-guide fence, and rout the innermost mortise to a depth of ⅝ in. (see photo C on p. 150). When

routing the 1⅜-in.-long mortises at the bottom of each leg, remove the ³⁄₁₆-in.-thick shims from the router-travel stops. Use them when cutting the 1¼-in.-long mortises at the top of each leg.

8. Rout the rest of the leg mortises in the same manner. Before you cut, always make sure that an inner face of the leg is against the face of the jig. Otherwise, your mortises will be offset to the wrong edge of the leg.

Boring and tapping the caster holes

1. Use your saved offcut from the leg to make a guide block for drilling the caster bolt hole in the bottom of each leg. Crosscut the offcut to 1 in. long.

A MORTISING JIG

Routing mortises for loose-tenon joinery can present a bit of a challenge. Although it's easy enough to rout the edge mortises using a router edge guide, cutting the end mortises can be tricky because of the limited bearing surfaces for the router base and edge guide. Bill Hylton's mortising jig solves the problem and allows you to rout the edge mortises and end mortises with the same basic setup. This jig is particularly useful when routing twin mortises, such as those found on this tool cabinet.

In use, the jig holds the workpiece in the proper orientation for routing. When routing edge mortises, the workpiece is clamped to the face of the jig, resting on a horizontal work holder. When routing end mortises, the workpiece is clamped to a vertical work holder. Adjustable stops on the top of the jig can

be set to restrict the amount of router travel. A track at the rear of the jig allows the use of a shim to offset the mortises, rather than having to reset the edge guide.

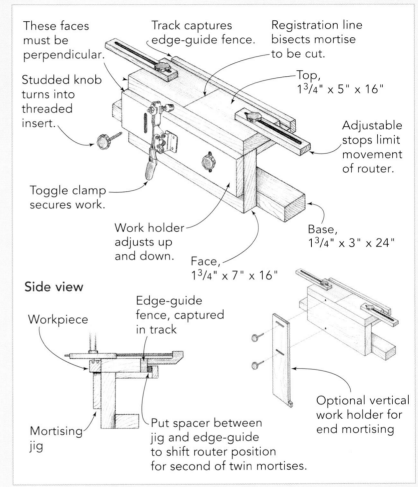

These faces must be perpendicular.

Studded knob turns into threaded insert.

Track captures edge-guide fence.

Registration line bisects mortise to be cut.

Top, 1³/4" x 5" x 16"

Adjustable stops limit movement of router.

Toggle clamp secures work.

Work holder adjusts up and down.

Base, 1³/4" x 3" x 24"

Face, 1³/4" x 7" x 16"

Side view

Workpiece

Edge-guide fence, captured in track

Mortising jig

Put spacer between jig and edge-guide to shift router position for second of twin mortises.

Optional vertical work holder for end mortising

2. Using a ²⁷/₆₄-in.-dia. bit in the drill press, bore a hole through the axis of the guide block.

3. Clamp the guide block to the end of each leg using a handscrew. Drill a 1½-in.-deep hole into the bottom of the leg using your ²⁷/₆₄-in.-dia. bit.

4. Using a tap for ½-in.-dia. holes, thread the bolt hole in each leg (see photo D on p. 150). You can get a tap at the hardware store for just a few dollars.

Shaping the bottom rails

1. Make the two templates for routing the curved bottom rails (see the drawing "Rail Templates" on p. 150). Each template consists of a ¼-in.-thick MDF panel to which are attached ¾-in.-thick by 1-in.-wide fences for holding the workpiece when routing. To make the arc, trace along a thin, straight-grained piece of wood that has been sprung to the desired curve (see the drawing

Rail Templates

Side Rail Template

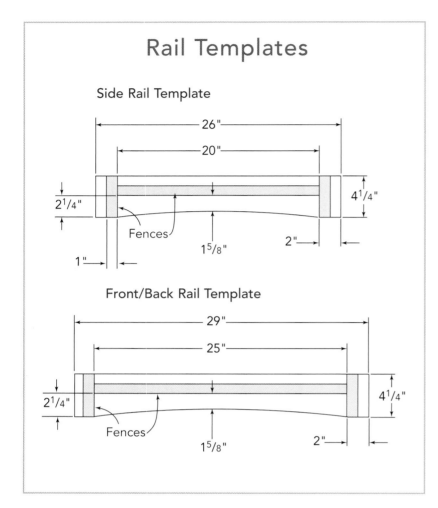

26"
20"
2¼"
4¼"
Fences
2"
1⁵⁄₈"
1"

Front/Back Rail Template

29"
25"
2¼"
4¼"
Fences
1⁵⁄₈"
2"

Springing a Curve

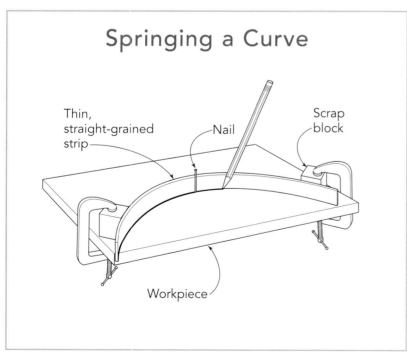

Thin, straight-grained strip

Nail

Scrap block

Workpiece

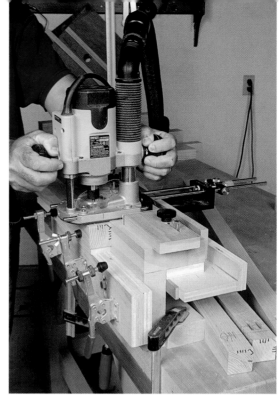

PHOTO C: When routing the mortises for the legs, mount the leg on top of the horizontal work holder and leave the router-travel stops set up as before. The ³⁄₁₆-in.-thick shims against the ends of the stops are removed when routing the longer of the twin mortises.

"Springing a Curve" at left). Cut the curves with a bandsaw or jigsaw, and smooth them fair using files and sandpaper.

2. Use the templates to lay out the curves on the rail blanks. Bandsaw the rails to within ¹⁄₁₆ in. of your line.

3. Mount each rail in its jig, and rout to the final profile (see photo E on facing page).

Making and fitting the loose tenons

1. Rip a length of 1¼-in.-wide stock and a length of 1⅜-in.-wide stock to make the tenons. Plane the stock for a snug fit in the mortises. You should be able to insert the tenons using just a bit of finger pressure.

2. Rout, plane, or sand a bullnose profile on both edges of the tenon stock.

3. Crosscut the pieces to length. Each twin tenon joint receives one 1¹⁵⁄₁₆-in.-long tenon and one 1⁹⁄₁₆-in.-long tenon. The shorter

PHOTO D: Thread the hole for each caster bolt using a tap

PHOTO E: After bandsawing close to the rail's curved cut line, use a template and pattern bit to rout to the final profile.

tenon is mitered on the end that inserts into the leg (see photo F).

Dry-fitting the frames and cutting the panels

1. Dry-assemble the legs and rails, inserting all of the loose tenons. Clamp the assembly together to make sure that all the parts line up properly and that the joints all pull up tight.

2. With the unit still clamped up, measure the openings for the side panels, back panel, and bottom (see photo G on p. 152). Measure carefully, as any gaps between the panels and their frames will be evident after assembly.

3. Lay out the dovetails on the ends of the top front rail (see the drawing "Joints" on p. 148). Cut the tails to shape using a bandsaw or small backsaw.

4. Position the rail on top of the legs, carefully aligning the rear edge of the rail with the rear edge of the leg. Trace the shape of the dovetails onto the tops of the legs.

5. Using a router, waste away most of the dovetail sockets. Use a sharp chisel to pare to your cut lines until the dovetail fits its sockets snugly.

6. Saw the panels to size using a good-quality blade to minimize tearout.

PHOTO F: The inner loose tenons are shorter than the outer tenons and are mitered on one end where they meet inside the leg.

PHOTO G: After dry-clamping the legs and rails, Hylton measures the openings to determine the measurements for the back, bottom, and side panels.

the inner faces of the legs and rails (see photo H on facing page).

5. Cut the biscuit slots in the panels, centering them across the edge (see photo I on facing page).

6. Use your biscuit joiner to cut the tabletop-clip slots in the top rails. Hylton cut the slots ¼ in. down from the top edges of the rails, then made his own tabletop clips to suit. You could also use commercially available metal clips, cutting the slots to suit them instead.

Assembling the Case

Now you're ready to glue the case together, working in stages. However, before performing every assembly step below, it's wise to dry-fit the subassemblies first to set your clamps and to rehearse your clamp-up procedures.

1. Begin by gluing up each side assembly. A good approach is to build it standing on edge. Lay a leg on the bench, and then glue one of the rails to it. Next attach the panel, and then glue on the opposing rail. Last, attach the opposite leg. Make sure that the assembly is square under clamp pressure and that it's lying flat on the bench while the glue cures.

2. Glue the front and back bottom rails to the bottom panel, carefully aligning the ends of the rails with the ends of the panel. Make sure that the rails are square to the faces of the panel so that the loose-tenon joints don't cock out of line with their mortises in the legs.

3. At this point, dry-clamp the pieces to see if you are able to assemble the rest of the unit in one operation. Some cross-clamping will be necessary, so your success probably depends on your collection of deep-throat clamps. If you're not sufficiently equipped, your next step is to glue the back panel to its rails. It may help to dry-clamp the sides in place for alignment purposes.

4. Finish up by clamping the side assemblies to the bottom, back, and rails. To help keep the cabinet square during clamp-up, attach

TIP

When clamping panels or rails to legs, make sure that the clamp screws are centered across the thickness of the workpieces to prevent the pieces from buckling under clamp pressure.

Laying out and cutting the biscuit joints

1. Lay out and cut the biscuit slots for attaching the bottom to its rails (about four biscuits per edge). Align the slots so that the top face of the bottom panel will line up with the top edges of the rails (see the drawing "Mobile Tool Cabinet" on p. 144).

2. Lay out the slot spacing for attaching the side and back panels to the rails and legs. Four to five biscuits per edge is fine.

3. Set your biscuit-joiner fence for cutting the slots in the rails and legs. Offset the slots so that the inner faces of the panels will be inset ½ in. from the inner faces of the legs and rails (see the drawing "Joints" on p. 148).

4. Cut the slots in the legs and rails, always referencing your biscuit-joiner fence against

PHOTO H: When cutting the biscuit slots in the rails and legs, always reference your biscuit-joiner fence against the inner faces of the pieces.

PHOTO I: Center the biscuit slots across the edges of all the panels.

the top front rail but don't glue it in place yet. It's easier to install the drawers without it in the way.

Making the Drawers

The drawer boxes are made from 9-ply Baltic birch plywood. Solid-wood drawer fronts are screwed to the boxes after the drawers are installed.

1. Cut the drawer-box parts to size, and mark the parts for orientation (see the drawing "The Triangle Marking System" on p. 14).

2. Cut the joints. Hylton routed the joints using a drawer-lock bit in his router table (see the sidebar "Routed Drawer Lock Joint" on pp. 154–55). However, you could use any joints you like.

3. Saw the ¼-in. by ¼-in. grooves ¼ in. up from the bottom edges to accept the drawer bottoms (see the drawing "Mobile Tool Cabinet" on p. 144).

4. Dry-assemble each drawer to check the fit of the joints and the bottom in its grooves. Glue up the boxes on a flat work surface. Make sure the drawers are square under clamp pressure.

Installing the Drawers

Hylton used heavy-duty, full-extension drawer slides to carry the weight of metal tools and to allow easy access to items at the rear of a drawer.

1. Begin by cutting the drawer-slide shims to size. These will create a mounting surface flush to the inside faces of the legs.

2. Predrill and countersink the shim along their centerlines for attaching them to the side panels with three 1-in., #6 dry-wall screws.

3. Drill pilot holes along the centerline for attaching the slides to the shims. Use a slide to determine the correct spacing for the holes.

4. Screw the drawer shims to the side panels. To ensure that they were perpendicular to the face of the cabinet, Hylton rested the shims on a supporting plywood panel held against the case side. He began by cutting the panel to the proper height for installing the top shim. After screwing the top pair of shims in place, he installed their slides and trimmed the support panel to the correct height for the next lowest shims (see photo J on p. 155).

ROUTED DRAWER LOCK JOINT

A routed drawer lock joint provides a quick way to make drawer joints that resist the stresses caused by pulling and slamming drawers. The interlocking joint is made using a single drawer lock bit mounted in a router table. The drawer fronts and backs are cut by feeding the pieces flat on the table. The sides are cut with the pieces standing on edge. The bit stays at the same height for both cuts. Only the fence needs to be adjusted for the cuts.

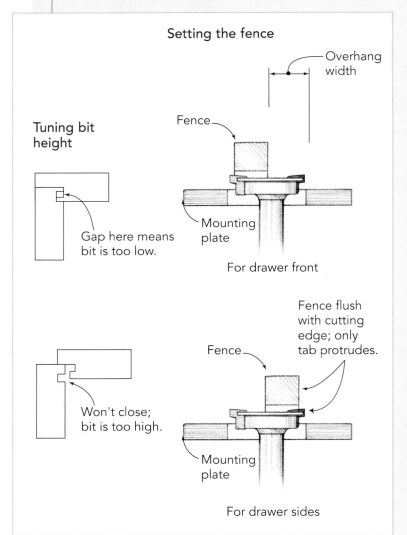

Setting the fence

Overhang width

Fence

Mounting plate

For drawer front

Tuning bit height

Gap here means bit is too low.

Fence flush with cutting edge; only tab protrudes.

Fence

Won't close; bit is too high.

Mounting plate

For drawer sides

Use scrap to set up the cuts. The first step is to set the bit height, as shown in the drawing at left, fine-tuning the height until there is no gap between the pieces. Next, set the fence for cutting the drawer front. The perimeter of the bit should protrude from the fence a distance equal to the thickness of the plywood. Set it as closely as you can, and make a test cut in scrap to check the depth of cut. When you've got it right, clamp registration blocks to the table behind the fence (see the top left photo on the facing page).

Finally, set the fence for cutting the drawer sides. The fence should be aligned with the lower section of the bit's cutting edge, as shown in the drawing. Only the tab section of the bit should protrude from the fence. Make a test cut, then clamp registration blocks in front of the fence (see the bottom photo on the facing page).

Make one last set of test cuts with the fence in both of its positions against the registration blocks. Fine-tune the fence settings if necessary and then cut your drawer joints.

PHOTO J: To keep the drawer-slide shims perpendicular to the case front, Hylton rests each shim on a square plywood panel pressed against the case side. Starting with the uppermost slides, he works downward, sawing the panel shorter to install each subsequent pair of shims.

5. Install the quick-disconnect rails to the drawer-box sides (see photo K on p. 156). The rails are offset on the drawer side because they ride on top of the extending slides. Space them so the drawer box will be centered on the telescoping drawer sides.

6. Now that the drawers are installed, you can glue the top front rail into its dovetail sockets.

Making and Attaching the Drawer Fronts

The drawer-front sizes listed in the cut list are ideal finished sizes. In fact, you'll cut the drawers about ⅟₁₆ in. oversize in width, and trim them to fit during installation.

1. Begin with the front for the bottom drawer, ripping it to about 7³⁄₁₆ in. wide. Before crosscutting it to length, check the square of

PHOTO K: A combination square gauges the lines for installing the quick-disconnect rails that attach to the drawer sides.

if fine, install the other screws. If the alignment is off, remove the installed screws, adjust the position of the front, and install the other two screws. When everything is aligned, drive all four screws home.

4. Install the rest of the drawer fronts moving upward in the same manner, using shims placed on the top edge of the drawer below.

5. After all the fronts are installed, use a sharp block plane to do any final edge trimming. Ease the sharp edges, and sand the drawer fronts through 220 grit.

Making and Attaching the Drawer Pulls

Hylton made his own wooden pulls. They align with the bottom edges of the drawers and increase in size from top to bottom. If you like, you could make the pulls all the same size or use commercial pulls instead.

1. Determine the lengths of the individual pulls by laying out lines from the center 11 in. of the top drawer downward to the bottom outside corners of the bottom drawer (see the drawing "Elevations" on p. 146).

2. Using the pull profiles' drawing as a reference, rip and plane lengths of stock slightly oversize in width (the pull height) and length for each pull. For example, the blank for the bottom pull would be $^{11}/_{16}$ in. thick by $1^{3}/_{8}$ in. wide by 27 in. long.

3. Rip the bevels on your table saw, with the bottom of the pull against the fence and the offcut underneath the tilted blade.

4. Set up your router table with a ¾-in.-dia. corebox bit, and rout the coved underside of each pull blank. Adjust your router fence for each pull so that you leave ⅛ in. of uncut wood at the nose of the pull.

5. Place each pull against its drawer front. Mark the trim lines on the ends of the pull, using the layout lines that you made on the drawer fronts as a reference.

6. Trim the ends of the pulls. To make the cuts, tilt your chopsaw blade to 45 degrees and set your miter angle to 13 degrees.

your case opening. If it's perfectly square, crosscut the drawer front to be ¹⁄₁₆ in. less than the opening. If the opening is out of square, crosscut the drawer front so it touches both stiles.

2. Place ¹⁄₁₆-in. shims on the case bottom, and clamp the drawer front to its box. Mark for trimming the ends (see photo J on p. 155). Aim for a gap of ³⁄₆₄ in. on each side. Use a sharp block plane to trim the end grain.

3. Reclamp the trimmed drawer front to the box. Remove the box, and drill four countersunk holes through the box to attach the front. Install two screws, remove the clamps, and recheck the fit in the case. If the alignment

MAKING DRAWER COMPARTMENTS

Drawers are a great storage solution because they can be built in sizes suitable to particular tools. They also provide easy access to items that might otherwise lie in piles on a shelf. But drawers full of small items can become a jumble of stuff to pick through. The best improvement you can make to such a drawer is to compartmentalize it with dividers.

Craig Bentzley outfits his tool cabinets with removable dividers that can be rearranged to suit his tool collection as needed. When making his drawers, he cuts ⅛-in.-wide slots in the drawer walls to accept dividers that are slotted to allow further compartmentalization. He makes the long main dividers from ¼-in.-thick solid wood, rabbeting them at their ends to slip into the slots in the drawer walls. The short dividers that connect to the long dividers are simply pieces of ⅛-in.-thick plywood.

You can retrofit any drawer for this type of system by first lining the walls of the drawer with slotted inserts to which you can add dividers as shown here.

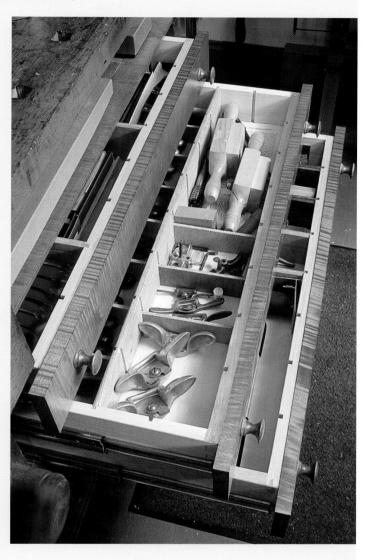

FRENCH-FIT DRAWERS

For the ultimate in organization, you can outfit tool-cabinet drawers with French-fit inserts, as Bill Hylton did. These inserts are simply panels cut out to accommodate specific tools. Hylton even applied flocking (see Sources on p. 172) to further protect and cushion his tools.

It's easy to make a French-fit drawer. Begin by cutting a panel to fit inside your drawer. You could use plywood, but MDF provides a cleaner, smoother surface. Hylton used ¼-in.-thick MDF, but you could use thicker material if deeper recesses would better serve your needs.

Lay your tools out on the panel and trace their profiles. Then cut the shapes using a jigsaw or scrollsaw. (Notice the semicircular cutouts for finger access incorporated in the recess for the metal rods.) Round over the edges, and use files and sandpaper to smooth and round in the corners where the bit can't reach. Glue the panel into the drawer, weighing it down with bricks or other heavy objects until the glue cures.

To apply flocking, paint the drawer with special flocking adhesive (see the photo at bottom left). Place the drawer in a plastic bag or canopy, and shoot the flocking onto the panel using a cardboard telescoping pump sold for the purpose (see the top photo at right). After the adhesive dries, brush away the excess flocking for one fine-looking drawer.

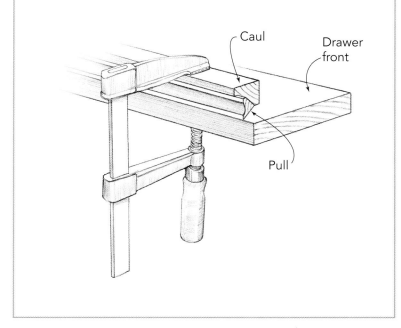

Clamping the Pulls

TO CLAMP THE BEVELED PULLS to the drawer fronts, make a clamping caul that complements the bevel and nose of the largest, lowermost pull. After attaching that pull, rip the caul to suit each successively smaller pull.

Caul

Drawer front

Pull

7. Sand the pulls, and clamp them to the drawer fronts. Hylton did this one at a time, starting with the lowermost pull and using a beveled clamping caul that he trimmed down for each successively smaller pull (see the drawing "Clamping the Pulls" on p. 159).

Finishing Up

1. Finish-sand the case, drawer fronts, and top.

2. Apply a finish. Hylton wiped on several coats of wiping varnish, sanding between coats.

3. Attach the top using tabletop clips. You can make your own, as shown in the drawing "Mobile Tool Cabinet" on p. 144, or use commercial metal clips.

The torsion box top of this mobile assembly table offers a dead-flat, glue-resistant, easily cleanable surface for assembling woodwork projects.

ASSEMBLY TABLE

ADEAD-FLAT ASSEMBLY TABLE can save a furniture maker untold grief. If the surface that you use to assemble projects isn't flat, it can introduce twist into your work, causing problems down the line with other subassemblies and installations. Most assembly tables that I've seen and used over the years have had tops made of MDF—and for good reason; MDF is about the flattest panel material around, and it's a great substrate for a plastic laminate covering, which is tough and glue resistant. Unfortunately, MDF—like all particleboard products—sags under its own weight over time. So even assembly tables with a good supporting framework underneath can sag between supports that aren't spaced closely together.

I decided to put the time into building an assembly table that would be dead flat and stay that way for the rest of my career. The solution was to make the top as a torsion box, which is comprised of a gridwork of closely spaced ribs sandwiched with glue between two panels. This creates a very stiff, rigid construction. The top is mounted on a low cabinet that provides a comfortable height for assembling medium-size cabinets and furniture.

I've used a number of mobile assembly tables that were outfitted with clamp drawers and overloaded with hardware and supplies to the point that calling them "mobile" was stretching the truth. I needed to be able to move my table around the shop more easily, so I purposely kept the case relatively lightweight and open, adding only a shelf or two. The compartments can be utilized as needed for tools and supplies.

If you're not concerned about mobility, you could eliminate the casters and simply extend the base to the floor. For storage, you could outfit the cabinet with drawers, shelves, or doors, as you like. Of course, you can make your assembly table any size you like, as well. Just make sure when you're designing the grid for the top that the next-to-outermost ribs overlay the top case frame for attaching the top.

ASSEMBLY TABLE

THE TORSION BOX TOP, with its MDF panels and internal grid of ribs, ensures a lifetime of flat stability. The plywood case, with its stiffening spine, can be outfitted with shelves or drawers for storage. The base supports the case and provides solid attachment for casters.

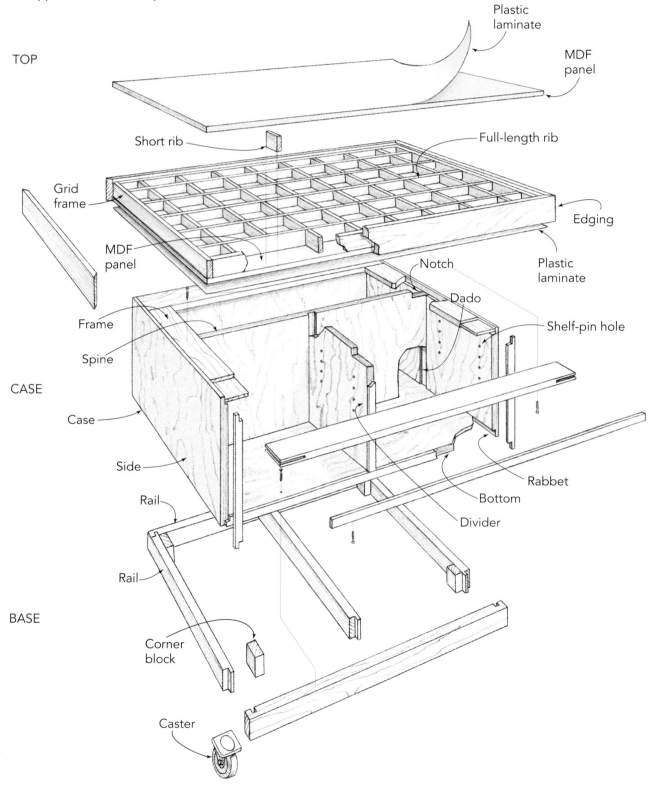

TOP

Plastic laminate

MDF panel

Short rib

Full-length rib

Grid frame

Edging

MDF panel

Plastic laminate

Notch

Dado

Shelf-pin hole

Frame

Spine

CASE

Case

Side

Rabbet

Bottom

Divider

Rail

Rail

BASE

Corner block

Caster

This project consists of three basic components: the base, the case, and the top (see the drawing "Assembly Table" on facing page). I built the base first so I could use it as a flat surface for assembling the top, which I made next. I put the case together last.

Making the Base

1. Rip and crosscut the stock for the base rails and corner blocks using dense, straight-grained hardwood. I used hard maple. Cut the pieces oversize in length and width, and let them relax for a few days before milling them to final size. Make extra stock for setting up cuts later.

2. Mark the pieces for orientation. I used the triangle marking system (see the drawing on p. 14).

3. Lay out the ½-in.-wide by ¾-in.-deep dadoes in the ends of the long rails to accept the tongues on the short rails.

4. Rout the dadoes. I clamped the two rails together and used a shopmade square to guide the router across both rails at once (see photo A).

5. Saw or rout the rabbets in the short rails to create the tongues that fit in the dadoes. Set up the cuts and test the fits using the extra stock you milled when making the rails. I made the cheek cuts first, using a tenoning jig on the table saw (see photo B

CUT LIST FOR ASSEMBLY TABLE			
Base			
2	Rails	1¾" x 2½" x 53"	Maple
3	Rails	1¾" x 2½" x 27"	Maple
2	Ledgers	1¼" x 1¼" x 25½"	Maple
4	Corner blocks	1¾" x 2½" x 3"	Maple
Top			
2	Panels	¾" x 35" x 60"	MDF
7	Ribs	¾" x 2¼" x 57½"	Pine
2	Ribs	¾" x 2¼" x 35"	Pine
32	Ribs	¾" x 2¼" x 6¼"	Pine
16	Ribs	¾" x 2¼" x 2⅜"	Pine
2	Edgings	½" x 3¾" x 36"	Maple
2	Edgings	½" x 3¾" x 60"	Maple
Cabinet			
2	Sides	¾" x 30½" x 15½"	Hardwood plywood
1	Spine	¾" x 14¾" x 54"	Hardwood plywood
1	Divider	¾" x 14¾" x 15⅛"	Hardwood plywood
1	Bottom	¾" x 30½" x 54"	Hardwood plywood
2	Cleats	¾" x 2" x 31"	Solid wood
2	Cleats	¾" x 2" x 54"	Solid wood
4	Edgings	¼" x ¾" x 15½"	Solid wood
2	Edgings	¼" x ¾" x 54"	Solid wood
1	Edging	¼" x ¾" x 15⅛"	Solid wood
Hardware			
4	Swivel casters	3"	Woodcraft, item #141051
16	Lag screws and washers	⁵⁄₁₆" x 1½"	

PHOTO A: Rout the dadoes in the base rails using a shopmade square to guide your router. For efficiency, gang the two rails together for the cut. (The extra edge joints you see here are a result of using butcher-block countertop for the rail stock.)

PHOTO B: The cheek cut for the rabbets was made using a shopmade tenoning jig on the table saw. The blade and fence have been set up using scrap, which was then test-fitted in the dado.

PHOTO C: The shoulder cut for the rabbet was made using the table-saw crosscut sled. The test piece cut for the previous step makes the perfect stop block, allowing space for the offcut to fall away.

on p. 164). I cut the shoulder using a stop block on my crosscut sled (see photo C).

6. Glue up the base on a flat surface, carefully aligning the edges of all the pieces. Sight across the top of the assembled base to make sure it's not twisted. If necessary, shim under the appropriate corners to make it flat. Let the assembly dry overnight.

7. After the glue dries, plane the edges flush to each other if necessary. This is important for proper case and caster attachment.

8. Cut the corner blocks to size and glue them to the base, carefully aligning them with the bottom edges of the base. The blocks will provide additional support and mounting for the casters.

Making the Top

Making the top isn't complicated, but it does require good material and accurate workmanship if you want to get a dead-flat surface. You don't have to use premium-grade pine for the ribs, but avoid pieces with squirrelly grain and a lot of knots, especially for the pieces used for the grid frame and full-length ribs.

Cutting the pieces to size

1. Make the rib stock, ripping the strips ¼ in. oversize in width. Sticker the pieces, and let them sit at least overnight to relax and do whatever warping they're going to do before further milling them.

2. Saw the MDF panels to 35¼ in. by 59¼ in. If you're frugal like me (my friends prefer the word "cheap"), you can get both panels from one sheet of MDF by abutting two pieces to make the bottom panel (see the drawing "MDF Panel Layout" on p. 166). Both the top and bottom panels will be trimmed flush to the grid frame after assembly.

3. After the rib stock has done whatever warping it's going to do, joint one edge of every piece straight and then rip all of the strips to 2¼ in. wide.

4. Crosscut the pieces to length, working as accurately as possible. After cutting one end of each piece square, use a stop block on your saw to ensure that all commonly sized ribs are exactly the same length.

Assembling the grid and panels

To put the top together, you'll assemble the grid of ribs, then glue and screw the two panels to the rib assembly.

1. To ensure that the top will be flat, it's important to work on a flat surface. To create one, place the base on a flat surface such as a benchtop, then sight across the top edges of the base to make sure it's sitting flat. Shim the corners if necessary. Then place your 35¼-in. by 59½-in. MDF panel on top of the base.

2. Working on the MDF panel, assemble the grid frame. First, nail or screw the corners together, carefully aligning all the edges. Then, nail or screw the full-length ribs in place, using the short ribs to space them the proper distance (see photo D on p. 166).

3. Using a large square laid across the full-length ribs, mark the layout lines for placing the short ribs (see the drawing "Elevations" on p. 167).

A LIFT FROM THE MEDICAL PROFESSION

When woodworker Walt Segl needed an assembly table, he used his connections with the medical industry to procure a surplus hospital-bed mechanism. Outfitting it with a maple butcher-block top provided him with an assembly table with built-in height adjust-

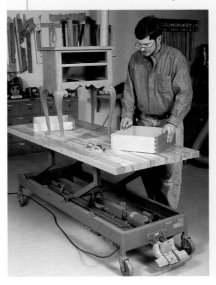

ment. Pressing a foot pedal raises the table to a height suitable for whatever-size project he's working on. Although not as rock-solid as a typical sturdy assembly table or workbench, Segl's assembly table is both mobile and convenient.

TORSION BOXES

A torsion box is a construction made by sandwiching a grid of closely spaced ribs between two panels. This yields an incredibly strong and rigid platform, and it's used in many applications where a supporting framework underneath the surface must be kept to a minimum. The top of many a large conference table is made of a torsion box, and it's a great solution for a shelf or countertop that needs to span a long area with no center support underneath.

The strength of a torsion box depends not only on the type and thickness of the wood used for the ribs and panels but also on the spacing of the ribs. The wood used for the ribs doesn't have to be dense for the torsion box to be strong. The box picks up a lot of strength from the fact that the ribs are glued to the panels, so using pine or another soft wood is usually fine, and it reduces the overall weight of the torsion box.

Closely spaced ribs add strength to the torsion box and minimize deflection of the panel areas between the ribs. Wider ribs increase the thickness of the torsion box and bolster its overall resistance to deflection. The grid of ribs consists of full-length pieces with short spacer ribs filling in between. It's usually best to run the full-length ribs the long dimension of the torsion box.

MDF Panel Layout

FOR ECONOMY, the bottom panel can be made by abutting two pieces cut to the sizes shown, yielding a seam that will straddle a rib in the torsion box top.

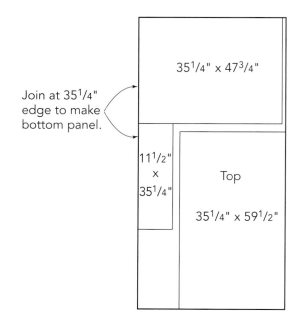

Join at 35¹/₄" edge to make bottom panel.

35¹/₄" x 47³/₄"

11¹/₂" x 35¹/₄"

Top

35¹/₄" x 59¹/₂"

PHOTO D: With the short ribs pressed against the frame between the full-length ribs, nail or screw through the outer frame into the end of each full-length rib.

PHOTO E: A staple straddling each short rib and full-length rib holds the pieces together. A bar clamp applies pressure across the assembly to ensure snug contact of the pieces.

TIP

Wood can contain internal stresses that are released after ripping a board, causing the newly sawn pieces to warp. To ensure that boards stay as straight and flat as possible over time, rip them about ¼ in. oversize in width, then sticker them for a day or so to let the pieces "relax" before jointing, planing, and ripping them to final size.

4. Arrange the short ribs in place, and staple them to the full-length ribs (see photo E). I used ⅜-in.-long staples. Hammer any proud staples flush into the surface. Afterward, carefully flip the grid over and staple the other side in the same manner.

5. Mark the centerlines of the long ribs onto the face of one of the MDF panels. Mark for screws along those lines, which should be spaced 7¼ in. apart.

6. Drill clearance holes through the MDF for the screws using a ⁵/₃₂-in.-dia. bit. Countersink the holes. Do *not* drill pilot holes into the ribs. Sand away any projecting blowout on the exit side of the holes.

7. Apply a coat of glue to the top edges of the ribs (see photo F on p. 168). It's best to use white—rather than yellow—glue for this because of the longer open-assembly time. Screw the panel to the grid using #6 by 1⅝-in. drywall screws. Before driving the screws, make sure that the panel overhangs the grid on all edges.

8. Flip the assembly over, mark the screw holes in the remaining panel, and drill them. Attach the panel with glue and screws in the same manner.

9. One important final step: Mark the locations of the perimeter screws on the edges of the top panel so you don't cut into them when cutting biscuit slots later. (Don't ask me how I found *this* out . . .)

Applying the plastic laminate

In the interest of balanced construction, I applied plastic laminate to the bottom of the

Elevations

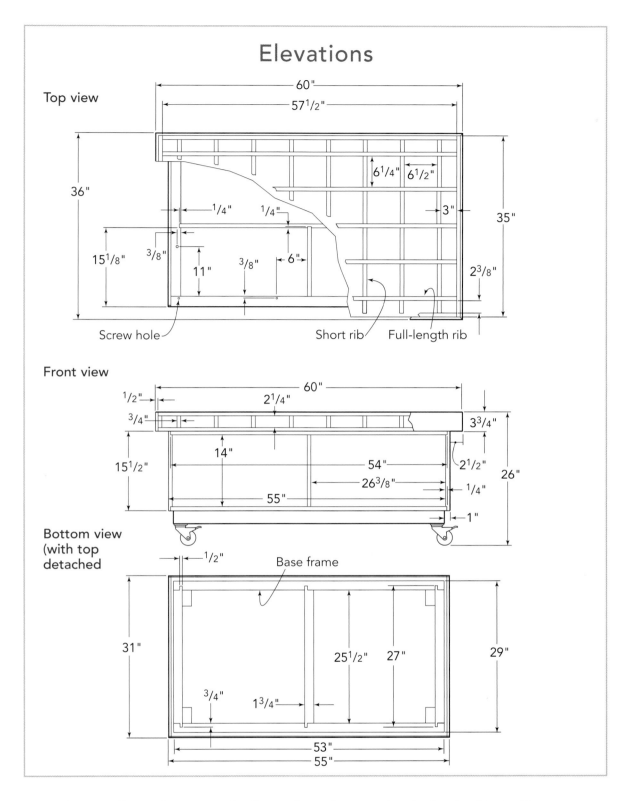

Top view

60"

57 1/2"

36"

35"

6 1/4" 6 1/2"

1/4" 1/4" 3"

15 1/8" 3/8" 3/8" 6" 2 3/8"

11"

Screw hole   Short rib   Full-length rib

Front view

1/2" 60"

2 1/4"

3/4" 3 3/4"

14" 54"

15 1/2" 26 3/8" 2 1/2" 26"

55" 1/4"

1"

Bottom view (with top detached

1/2"   Base frame

31" 25 1/2" 27" 29"

3/4" 1 3/4"

53"

55"

torsion box as well as to the top. I used a discounted sheet of damaged laminate on the bottom, but you could also piece together the bottom laminate using offcuts from the top sheet. If you want to make an auxiliary top for assembling shorter work, at a raised height this might be a good time to laminate

those pieces, too (see the drawing "An Auxiliary Top" on p. 169).

1. In preparation for applying the laminate, sand down any ridges on the panel caused by the countersink bit. Use compressed air to blow away the sanding dust to prevent contaminating the contact cement you'll use to apply the laminate.

PHOTO F: Use a small paint roller to apply white glue to the ribs for attaching the panel.

THE NODEN ADJUST-A-BENCH™

Woodworker Geoffrey Noden has developed what I consider to be one of the coolest innovations to come along in woodworking in recent years. The Adjust-A-Bench is a rock-solid assembly table/work-bench that easily adjusts in height from 28 in. to 45 in. Noden sells the metal trestles that incorporate the lifting mechanisms. You can attach whatever type of

benchtop you like to the trestles. Since using my Adjust-A-Bench, I've been amazed at how many times I change its height during the course of a workday—often raising it up for cutting dovetails, then dropping it down low for assembling cases. It's a real convenience, not to mention a back saver. (See "Sources" on p. 170.)

2. Apply contact cement to the MDF panel and to the laminate. I found that I had to apply a second coat to the porous MDF because it showed dry spots after tacking up.

3. After the contact cement tacks up, lay long dowels across the MDF panel and then place the laminate on top of the dowels, ensuring that the laminate meets or over-hangs the MDF panel at all edges.

4. Working from the center of the panel, press the laminate onto the MDF panels, removing the dowels as you work outward (see the top photo on p. 118). After removing all the dowels, apply heavy pressure to the entire surface using a roller, straight-sided glass jar, or piece of thick wood with a bull-nose edge.

5. Using a flush-trim router bit, trim the edges of the laminated MDF panel flush with the edges of the rib grid.

6. Flip the assembly over, and apply the lam-inate to the other side in the same manner. Trim those edges flush.

Fitting and applying the edging

1. Mill the stock for the edging, making sure it's a bit wider than the top is thick.

2. Fit the edging to the top, carefully miter-ing the ends to meet neatly (see photo G on facing page).

3. Cut the biscuit slots for attaching the edg-ing to the MDF panel (see photo H on facing page). These biscuits are more for alignment than joint strength. The slots will allow just enough up-and-down adjustment to push the edging a hair proud of the laminate when gluing it in place.

4. Glue the edging to the top, applying plenty of glue to the absorbent MDF edges. I clamped the edging in place, but you could nail or screw it instead. I attached the long pieces first, carefully aligning them at the corner using the dry-fit short pieces. After the glue dried, I attached the short pieces, making sure to apply glue to the faces of the miters.

5. Trim the edging flush to the laminate using a sharp block plane set for a very fine cut.

6. Rout a roundover on the edges and corners of the top using a ¼-in.-radius roundover bit.

Making the Case

The case is a simple construction consisting of two sides, a bottom, a spine, a compartment divider, and a frame. I used dadoes to align and connect the spine to the sides and to connect the divider to the spine. You could use biscuits instead, but remember to adjust the sizes of the pieces accordingly.

Preparing the plywood pieces

1. Lay out the plywood pieces, all of which can be cut from one sheet of plywood.

2. Cut the bottom and sides to size, ripping away the plywood factory edge in the process. Rip the spine and divider to 15 in. for now, but crosscut them to finished length. During the assembly process, you'll rip them to exactly match the height of the sides.

3. Mill and apply ¼-in.-thick edging to the sides, bottom, and divider. Make the edging slightly wider than the thickness of the plywood, and trim it flush after gluing it on (see the photos on p. 127).

An Auxiliary Top

FOR WORKING ON shorter projects without bending over, you can raise the height of your assembly table with this auxiliary top. The knock-down riser can be disassembled and stored in the long compartment of your assembly table. If you cover the top with plastic laminate, be sure to cover the panel bottom as well to prevent warping.

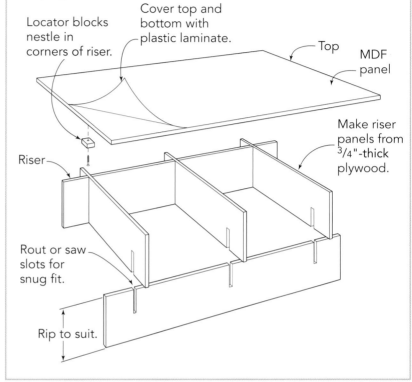

Locator blocks nestle in corners of riser.

Cover top and bottom with plastic laminate.

Top

MDF panel

Riser

Make riser panels from ³/4"-thick plywood.

Rout or saw slots for snug fit.

Rip to suit.

PHOTO G (far left): When fitting the mitered edging to the top, clamp two adjacent pieces to the top with their miters meeting neatly at the corner. Care-fully mark the opposite miters with a miter square and a sharp pencil.

PHOTO H (near left): To provide support for the biscuit-joiner fence when slotting the edging, orient the edging inside out and clamp it to the edge of the top.

PHOTO I: Using a tenoning jig and a dado head, cut the open-mortise half of each joint. Set up the saw and test the cut using scrap.

PHOTO J: Again using scrap to set up the cut, adjust the rip fence and cut the first cheek on all tenons. Next, slide the rip fence over to make all of the second cheek cuts.

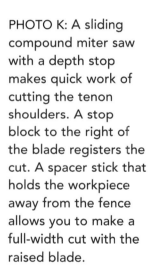

PHOTO K: A sliding compound miter saw with a depth stop makes quick work of cutting the tenon shoulders. A stop block to the right of the blade registers the cut. A spacer stick that holds the workpiece away from the fence allows you to make a full-width cut with the raised blade.

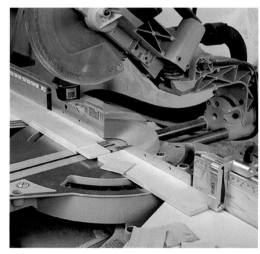

Making the frame

1. Mill the pieces for the top frame. Make extra stock to use for setting up the joint cuts.

2. Make the corner joints. I used bridle joints, which make for great strength (see photos I, J, and K). However, you could join the corners with biscuits, dowels, or simple half-lap joints.

3. Glue up the frame on a flat surface, such as your brand spankin' new assembly table-top. Compare the diagonals to make sure the frame is square after clamping.

4. Orient the plywood pieces for good looks, and mark them using the triangle marking system (see the drawing on p. 14).

5. Lay out the dadoes in the sides and spine.

6. Saw or rout the dadoes, after setting up the cut using scrap.

7. Cut the rabbets in the bottom edges of the sides. The width of the rabbets should exactly match the thickness of the bottom.

8. You need to measure for the final width of the spine. To do this, first dry-clamp the spine and one of the sides to the bottom. Then make a mark near the top edge of the spine where it meets the side. Rip the spine to the mark to ensure that it is exactly the same height as the sides.

9. Cut the rabbets in the top edge of the sides, exactly matching the width of the rabbet to the thickness of the frame.

10. Cut the notches in the spine and divider to accept the frame. I used a jigsaw, but you could cut them using a table saw.

Assembling the case

1. Lay out the screw holes for attaching the divider to the spine. Glue and screw the divider into its dado, carefully aligning the edges of the spine and divider. I used #6 by 2-in. drywall screws.

2. Lay out the screw holes for attaching the bottom to the spine and divider. Drill a clearance hole through the bottom for each screw. There is no need to countersink the holes, as the head will pull itself down into the plywood surface.

3. Glue and screw the bottom to the spine and divider (see photo L on facing page).

4. Flip the unit right side up. With the sides clamped lightly to the spine, glue and screw the top frame to the spine and divider. One screw at each notch will do the trick.

5. Attach the sides. I glued and clamped them, but you could either glue and nail or screw them instead, filling the holes later if you like.

6. Drill the shelf-pin holes using a brad-point bit to minimize tearout. I used a shopmade plywood drilling template to guide the bit.

7. Screw the case to the base using 2-in.-long screws. For each screw, drill a pilot hole into the base and a clearance hole through the case to ensure good contact between the pieces. If you want to plug the holes for looks, as I did, drill counterbores as well and plug the holes later.

8. If you're going to apply finish to the case, it's easier to do it now, before attaching the top.

9. Attach each caster using four ⁵⁄₁₆-in. by 1½-in. lag screws. I installed flat washers as well (see photo M). I set the caster plate about ⁵⁄₁₆ in. in from the edges of the base.

10. Attach the case to the top with #8 by 2½-in. drywall screws driven into the ribs (see the drawing "Elevations" on p. 167). For good screw purchase, I drilled pilot holes through the MDF panel (but *not* into the ribs) and drilled clearance holes through the frame and plastic laminate.

11. With a helper, flip the unit right side up and roll it to your assembly area. Your workmanship is about to move up a notch.

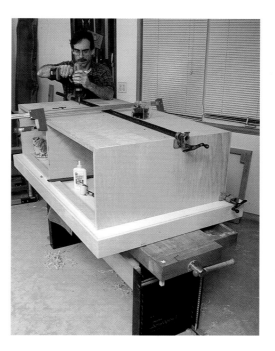

PHOTO L: With the sides dry-clamped to the spine and with the unit upside down, glue and screw the bottom to the spine and divider using #6 by 2-in. drywall screws.

RETROFITTING FOR MOBILITY

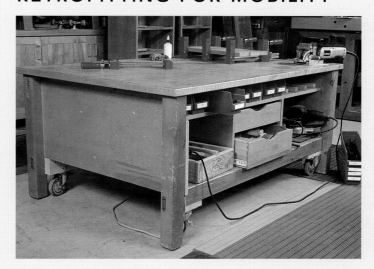

When Andy Rae moved to a larger shop, he found that he needed to be able to move around his previously stationary assembly table. So he added L-shaped blocks to the lower rails and affixed casters to the unit. A heavy assembly table like this—with its thick posts and rails, MDF panels, and load of tools and hardware—requires heavy-duty casters. Don't stint on their cost.

PHOTO M: Attach the casters to the base using lag screws and washers.

SOURCES

ADJUST-A-BENCH
Geoffery Noden
232 Stokes Ave.
Trenton, NJ 08638
(609) 882-3300
www.geocities.com/adjustabench/
Adjustable bench hardware

HARTVILLE TOOL
940 W. Maple St.
Hartville, OH 44632
(800) 345-2396
www.hartvilletool.com
*T-track, hardware, tools, and
woodworking supplies*

LEE VALLEY TOOLS LTD.
PO Box 1780
Ogdensburg, NY 13669
(800) 871-8158
www.leevalley.com
*Hardware, tools, and woodworking
supplies*

LIE-NIELSEN TOOLWORKS, INC.
PO Box 9
Warren, ME 04864
(800) 327-2520
www.lie-nielsen.com
Exceptional handplanes

MICRO FENCE
11100 Cumpston St., #35
N. Hollywood, CA 91601
(800) 480-6427
www.microfence.com
Exceptional router edge guides

REID TOOL SUPPLY CO.
2265 Black Creek Rd.
Muskegon, MI 49441
(800) 253-0421
www.reidtool.com
*Handles, knobs, tool, and
woodworking supplies*

ROCKLER WOODWORKING
AND HARDWARE
4365 Willow Dr.
Medina, MN 55340
(800) 279-4441
www.rockler.com
*Knobs, flocking supplies, hardware,
tools, and woodworking supplies*

WOODCRAFT
PO Box 1686
Parkersburg, WV 26102
(800) 225-1153
www.woodcraft.com
*Minitrack, casters, hardware, tools,
and woodworking supplies*

WOODHAVEN
501 W. First Ave.
Durant, IA 52747
(800) 344-6657
www.woodhaven.com
*Router-table fences, hardware, and
router accessories*

WOODWORKER'S HARDWARE
PO Box 180
Sauk Rapids, MN 56379
(800) 383-0130
www.wwhardware.com
*Drawer slides, pulls, hinges, tools,
and woodworking supplies*

WOODWORKER'S SUPPLY, INC.
1108 N. Glenn Rd.
Casper, WY 82601
(800) 645-9292
www.woodworker.com
*Hardware, tools, and woodworking
supplies*

WOODWORKING FASTTRAK, INC.
W5823 School Ave.
Merrill, WI 54452
(888) 327-7725
www.woodworkingfasttrak.com
*T-track, flip stops, and
woodworking-machine
accessories*